THE PICTORIAL
HISTORY OF THE
HOLOCAUST

THE PICTORIAL HISTORY OF THE HOLOCAUST

Edited by

YITZHAK ARAD

Designed by Hava Mordohovich

YAD VASHEM
The Holocaust Martyrs' and Heroes'
Remembrance Authority
JERUSALEM

MACMILLAN PUBLISHING COMPANY
NEW YORK
Collier Macmillan Publishers
LONDON

THE PUBLICATION OF THIS ALBUM HAS BEEN MADE POSSIBLE THROUGH
THE INITIATIVE AND GENEROSITY OF MIRIAM AND HAIM SCHÄCHTER

Editorial Board: Yitzhak Arad, Reuven Dafni, Gideon Greif, Yehudit Levin

All photos © Yad Vashem, Jerusalem, except for:
Henning Langenheim, Berlin (West): photos 292, 293, 295, 299
Bildarchiv Abraham Pisarek, Berlin (West): photos 33, 34, 35, 36, 37, 38, 39, 40
Bundes Archiv, Koblenz: photo 135
Steidel Verlag, Goettingen: photos 145, 147, 152, 153, 154, 156, 157, 163,164, 171, 173, 174,
    175, 176
Yitzhak Kerem, Jerusalem: photo 382
Maps drawn by Alisa Gold

English language edition published by
Macmillan Publishing Company
A Division of Macmillan, Inc.

Macmillan Publishing Company   Yad Vashem
866 Third Avenue   P.O.B. 3477
New York, NY 10022   Jerusalem 91034, Israel

Library of Congress Catalog Card Number: 90-6044
Printed in Israel
Printing Number
1 2 3 **4** 5 6 7 8 9 10 - Printed in 1994

Library of Congress Cataloging-in-Publication Data

The Pictorial History of the Holocaust / edited by Yitzhak Arad;
designed by Hava Mordohovich; Yad Vashem, The Holocaust Martyrs'
and Heroes' Remembrance Authority, Jerusalem

    p.   cm.
ISBN 0-02-897011-X
I. Holocaust, Jewish (1939–1945)—Pictorial works.   1. Arad, Yitzhak,
1926–   II. Yad Vashem, Rashut Hazikaron la-Shoah ve la-Gevurah.
D804.3.P53   1990
940.53'18'0222-- cd20   90-8044
                    CIP

The indescribable atrocities committed by Nazi Germany while the free world stood passively by are portrayed graphically in this album. The reader is confronted by hundreds of photographs, among them many of children at a loss to comprehend the terrible wrong afflicted on them and the reason for their suffering. These sights should remain engraved indelibly on our consciousness.

The Nazis, who perpetrated some of the most gruesome crimes in history, were not barbarians but ordinary human beings who succumbed to their most bestial instincts. Germany, one of the most cultured of the western nations, whose poets, writers, painters, composers and scientists had enriched and inspired the civilized world, was at the same time the birthplace of Nazism. Six million Jews, of whom one-and-a-half million were children, were murdered in the Nazi attempt to annihilate the Jewish nation — a nation that had bequeathed to the world the belief in one God, the principles of justice and righteousness, and the sublime vision of peace as expressed by the Prophet Isaiah: "Nation shall not lift up sword against nation, neither shall they learn war any more."

This album should serve as a warning that the fruits of civilization alone cannot constitute a protection against human savagery: the underlying values and significance of culture and civilization must become deeply ingrained in each and every human being, an organic part of his inner self. As the prophet Jeremiah said: "I will put my law in their inward parts and write it in their hearts" (Jer. 31:33). Only man's personal identification with the essence of culture and morality can ensure that he possesses the necessary attitude of responsibility with respect to his actions.

The aim of this album is to demonstrate to what depths mankind can sink, in the hope that we may in future be induced to conquer our bestial nature and allow a more spiritual light to illuminate our path. Thus we may eliminate the possibility of any recurrence of the atrocities perpetrated during the Holocaust.

Haim Schächter

The Holocaust, *Shoah* in Hebrew, is the most tragic era in the history of the Jewish people – 1933 and 1945 – when the Germans and their collaborators perpetrated genocide against them. By the end of the Second World War, the Nazis and their minions had managed to put some six million Jews to death and destroy thousands of Jewish communities. Cultural and material assets built with great labor and care over centuries – were burned and destroyed.

This album has been created as the pictorial history of the Shoah. Its photographs depict the humiliation, abuse, suffering, and death that were the lot of the Jews in the territories under the rule of Nazi Germany and its allies in occupied Europe. They show the unspeakable crimes committed by the Nazis against human beings – men and women, young and old – whose sole offense was having been born Jews. The hatred of Jews, anti-Semitism, that had for years been cultivated in Christian society, both in Germany and in other European countries, laid the ground for these crimes and enabled them to take place on a scope previously unknown in the civilized world. Even the Jewish people, schooled in suffering, expulsions, pogroms, and murder for generations, had never in its long history known death and mayhem on such a scale.

The Nazis' crimes against the Jews were the work not of individuals, groups, or even wild, incited mobs but of agencies of the state. They were committed in the name of an ideological doctrine – Nazi racism – and executed according to pragmatic plans that had been prepared in advance and were known by the catch-all "The Final Solution of the Jewish Problem." Involved in the planning, the deportations, and the number of the Jews were people from all quarters of the German regime: the Nazi party and the civil service, the S.S. and the *Wehrmacht*, the railway system, the local authorities, the media – each and every one. Among the commanders of the murder units at the trenches of slaughter and in the extermination camps were members of the intelligentsia, professors and physicians. The Nazis found local collaborators who took part in the deportation and extermination of Jews throughout Europe. They used barbarous terror against other peoples as well, and millions of innocent souls perished at their hands; but to only one people, to the Jews, did they apply the comprehensive program of the "Final Solution," whose aim was the systematic murder and utter obliteration of them from the face of the earth.

This album shows both the murderers and torturers in action and the Jews in their struggle for life; their fight to preserve their dignity under the harrowing conditions of the ghettos and camps; their efforts to continue educating their children; their struggle against hunger and disease; and their resolve to practice the Jewish religion and uphold its traditions. They are shown fighting in the ghetto uprisings and as partisans in the forests. However, since the photographs are limited to what transpired in the countries of Europe under Nazi domination, they do not show any of the hundreds of thousands of Jews who fought in the ranks of the Allied armies – a subject worthy of an album of its own.

Assembling the photographs for this book, and especially those showing the acts of murder and extermination, was no mean task. For the Germans tried to conceal their crimes against the Jewish people, and to that end they issued a strict prohibition against photographing the mass executions perpetrated by the *Einsatzgruppen* and other units; life in the concentration camps and even more so the death inflicted in the extermination camps, the death marches and all the other savage deeds they performed. The German soldiers serving in the extermination camps were obliged to sign a vow that they would not take pictures. The Jews in the ghettos, camps and forests did not have access to cameras. Nevertheless, occasionally these crimes were immortalized on film. In some cases Germans themselves took photographs covertly or with permission; in others it was soldiers from the Axis armies fighting alongside Germany – Italians, Hungarians, and others – who photographed the events they witnessed. There were also members of various undergrounds and other local inhabitants who dared to take pictures; and finally there were Jews who, literally at peril to their lives, saved or obtained photographic equipment and documented the Nazis' deeds in this way. Still, there are certain subjects, areas, and even whole countries on which there are hardly any photographs depicting the fate of the Jews or of which only photographs of very poor quality survived, making it impossible to include them in this album.

Despite all the difficulties, however, assembled here is a comprehensive collection of photographs – some rare, others published for the first time – that chart in chronological succession the various stages of the "Final Solution." The pictures in this book speak for themselves, and the accompanying captions are designed to provide only information not directly conveyed by them. The album also contains a comprehensive and up-to-date historical survey of the Shoah, filling in the narrative of the events as an aid to understanding their reflection in the photos. The book is divided into four periods in accordance with the historical phases of the Holocaust:

1933–1939: The persecution of the Jews within the Third Reich, including some brief background on the history of anti-Semitism.

1939–1941: The German conquest of most of Europe, the incarceration of the Jews in ghettos, and their exploitation as slave labor, along with other manifestations of brutal abuse.

1941–1945: The mass murder of the Jews and their resistance in the ghettos or as partisans in the forests.

1945–1948: The liberation of the camps, the surviving Jews, and their determined efforts to reach Eretz-Israel (Palestine).

The purpose of this album is not only to recount events or to inform its readers of the facts of the Holocaust. It is also meant to serve as a warning against continued expressions of enmity, acts of cruelty that are still occurring today in the world, and the specific phenomenon of anti-Semitism, which we so hoped, after all that had happened during the Holocaust, would vanish entirely. Wherever anti-Semitism exists, the basic values of enlightened society – tolerance, liberty, and the dignity of man – are inevitably trampled upon. Wherever the hatred of Jews has been commended or practiced as an official or semi-official policy, values such as democracy and liberalism were always at a nadir. This is a lesson we all should remember well.

The photographs presented in the following pages come mostly from the Yad Vashem Archives, with some being taken from private collections and from books. I should like to express my thanks to all those who have aided in the preparation of this album.

Yitzhak Arad

CONTENTS

Introduction/5
Foreword/7
Nazism and its Origins/13
Persecution of Jews in Germany 1933–1939/31
European Jews under Nazi Rule and Terror 1939–1941/65
The Ghettos/97
Mass Murder/171
Deportations to Death Camps/203
The Death Camps/251
Jewish Armed Resistance in Occupied Europe/319
Partisans/335
End of the War/359
En Route to Israel/383

NAZISM AND ITS ORIGINS

NAZISM AND ITS ORIGINS

Origins of Christian Anti-Semitism

Jewish presence in Europe goes back many generations. At the close of the first millenium C.E., the prevailing majority of the Jewish people in the world lived on the continent. For the next thousand years, until the Holocaust, Europe was the material and spiritual center of world Jewry. With the Holocaust this center ceased to exist.

To a considerable degree the situation and status of European Jews coincide with the history of conflict between the idea of tolerance toward them on the one hand, and the trend toward persecution and oppression originating in the Christian Church, on the other. As the influence of the Church in Europe grew, the trend toward persecution gradually gained the upper hand over the idea of tolerance. According to the basic view held by the Church, the oppressed and despised Jew provided living proof of the truth of Christianity. His inferior status, so the argument went, could be construed as a punishment for having dared to reject God incarnate — Jesus Christ. Consequently, the Jews must live as outcasts, branded with the stigma of Cain, until the day they would acknowledge the truth of God and His messiah. A vivid illustration of this idea can be found in medieval iconography in which two female figures were juxtaposed: one, representing a glorious and victorious Church, the other, blindfolded, symbolizing the oppressed Jewish Synagogue.

Propagation of such views by the Church for hundreds of years, particularly by rank-and-file clergy, could not but leave a deep mark on the attitude of the Christian populace toward the Jews. These attitudes, in turn, gave rise to violence, persecutions and blood libels which were to characterize Jewish-Christian relations for centuries. The long history of persecution is replete with episodes in which Jews were signaled out as scapegoats, particularly during the Crusades, the Black Plague, wars, and times of natural calamities in their countries of residence. Christian demonology portrayed them

1. Blood libel. A woodcut of 1475 from Trinetto, Italy, where Jews were accused of murdering a Christian boy to use his blood for ritual purposes.

as murdering Christian children for ritual purposes, desecrating the host, poisoning the wells, and worshipping the Devil. During the Middle Ages in the countries of Western and Central Europe, time and again they were offered a choice between conversion and exile.

Thousands of Jews perished in popular outbursts and riots, scores of thousands underwent forcible conversions, while others met their death on the stakes of the Inquisition. Hundreds of thousands, having been expelled from the lands wherein they had lived for centuries, wandered from one country to another in search of refuge. Toward the close of the medieval period, after the ordeal of expulsions and wanderings, the majority of the Jewish people on the continent were concentrated in the countries of Eastern and Central Europe. Despite all the economic and physical onslaughts against them, the overwhelming majority of the Jewish people remained loyal to their religion and retained their national identity.

Having rebuilt their homes and communities in their new haven the Jews had not left their hardships behind them. Jew-hatred, rooted in the religious tradition, and their status as outcasts banned from associating with Christians, closed before them many occupations and whole spheres of economic activity. A Jew could not own or lease arable land, was prohibited from bearing arms, was excluded from membership in merchant and craftsmen associations (guilds) that controlled various areas of trade, etc. Christian society made available to Jews only those occupations it regarded as contemptible: usury, tax collecting among the peasants on behalf of the landowner, itinerant peddling, etc. The concentration of Jews in these occupations contributed

2. Blood libel. A 15th century woodcut from Germany showing Jews with the circular Jewish badge of identification extracting blood from the infant Simon's body.

3. Blood libel. A woodcut of 1591 from Pressburg (Bratislava) in the Austro-Hungarian Empire. Jews were accused of stealing the Eucharist; the woodcut depicts their fate.

3

14

further to anti-Jewish sentiments. Thus, the old anti-Semitism rooted in religious tradition was now overlaid with Jew-hatred stemming from the singular economic role played by the Jews in Christian society.

Political anti-Semitism

Ideas of egalitarianism propagated by the French Revolution together with the ideology of liberalism spawned by the 19th century brought about remarkable changes in the situation and status of the Jews. Emancipation brought in its wake equal rights for Jews in most European countries. The energies, resourcefulness and industry which had been pent up in Jewish society living within the walls of ostracism erected by Christendom now burst into the open. Jews eagerly seized on the equality of opportunities offered to them and within a relatively short time made immense strides in many fields of endeavor, primarily in the countries of Western and Central Europe. However, this process stopped short of their absorption into the surrounding society. Besides liberalism, the 19th century also gave birth to such influential ideologies as romanticism and nationalism. Broadly conceived, the movements inspired by these ideas regarded nations and their historical and cultural traditions as the fountainhead of communal existence and exhorted their compatriots to return to them. An offshoot of this view was that anyone who did not belong to the indigenous national collectivity by virtue of having descended from it and having been reared in its own unique values, was regarded as a foreign implant in the body of the nation and its political instrument — the national state. However, the traditions, values and religion of the Jews clearly set them apart from the peoples in whose midst they dwelled. Romanticism and nation-

4. Anti-Semitic caricature showing the Jew working behind the scenes of superpower struggles and meddling in world affairs. The poster reads: "Behind the hostile powers: the Jew."

5. "The Eternal Jew" — a poster for a Nazi film made in 1940.

alism went to great lengths to underscore this alien quality of the Jews within European societies which not so long before had opened their gates to them.

From the mid-19th century on, the rapid economic and social advancement of the alien Jew, the outcast of yesterday, in conjunction with the formation of a Jewish capitalist class, a negligible minority within the Jewish populace, deepened the hatred and envy of the Jews. Even liberal and socialist circles were not exempt from these sentiments. In total disregard of the fact that the overwhelming majority of the Jewish people struggled for subsistence in conditions of dire poverty, some socialist and marxist movements propagated the class hatred of the financier — the "Jewish capitalist." At the same time, nationalistic and reactionary circles regarded the hateful socialism and marxism as ideologies disseminated by the Jews aimed at demolishing the traditional human community. Marx's own Jewish origins, despite the intensely anti-Jewish sentiments evident in his writings, served to reinforce this line of anti-Semitic propaganda. Anti-Semitism assumed a political guise which attacked the Jews as carriers and disseminators of destructive political and class ideologies. These accusations launched both by the right- and left-wing extremes of the political spectrum contributed further to hatred of the Jews.

Racism

In the second half of the 19th century a new school of social and scientific thought evolved which added yet another dimension to the old anti-Semitism. The idea of racial theory was founded on the premise of inequality between various races and conceived of humankind as divided into racial groups exhibiting markedly different traits. These traits, in turn, were allegedly determined by various anthropological elements, mental characteristics and blood type. By likening the processes occuring in human societies to natural evolution, in the course of which the stronger types survive by preying on the weaker, human history was portrayed as a scene of struggle between various races. Out of the incessant, bloody struggle for survival, the stronger, more talented and successful races emerge victorious over the weaker, unproductive and degenerate ones which either disappear or become slaves of their victors. Such views practically did away with the uniqueness of man in the animal kingdom. Human reason and morality were held as inconsequential when compared with brute force and survivability. The commandment "Thou shall not kill," bequeathed to the world by Judaism, was rendered null and void.

Racial theories quickly acquired anti-Semitic overtones. In this interpretation the Aryan race to which the German people belonged constituted the apex of the pyramid of human races. This particular race was held as a source of all that is productive, good and creative in the world. Jews, on the other hand, occupied the lowest rung in the ladder of races. According to this view, all corruption, evil and parasitism derived and originated from them. Furthermore, racial traits were held as innate, i.e., present at birth in the individual's blood, and thus immutable. Consequently, a Jew who tried to assimilate, convert, or marry a non-Jewish spouse remained a Jew. More than that, his attempts to intermix with the Aryan races would corrupt Aryan blood and therefore must be combatted. Thus racial theories gave rise to racial anti-Semitism — hatred of Jews on the basis of their racial characteristics, coupled with the view that by their very presence the Jews defiled other races and endangered their purity.

The hope that the ideas of progress, liberalism, and socialism, together with emancipation, would solve the problems besetting the Jews failed to materialize. The trial of Alfred Dreyfuss, a Jewish officer in the General Staff of the French army, threw into bold relief the situation of the Jews before whom the Emancipation was supposed to remove all obstacles to entry into non-Jewish society. Dreyfuss was held on trumped-up charges of having passed secret documents of the French General Staff to the Germany Embassy in Paris. At his trial in 1895, judges of the military court, prejudiced against the officer whose Jewish origins set him apart from his French comrades-in-arms, found Dreyfuss guilty, demoted him and sentenced him to jail. After three years of stormy judicial battle which aroused public passions in France to an unprecedented degree, Dreyfuss was acquitted. It came to light that he had been framed by a group of anti-Semitic French officers. After lengthy deliberations in a number of judicial instances, Dreyfuss was ultimately released. The anti-Semitic background of this trial sent shock waves throughout the Jewish world, alerting the Jewish masses to the fact that the Emancipation had fallen short of solving their problems.

Pogroms in East Europe

Unlike its Western and Central European counterparts, anti-Semitism in Eastern Europe in general, and in Czarist Russia in particular, assumed the most violent forms. Toward the close of the 19th century and the first two decades of the 20th, Russian Jewry was swept by a wave of pogroms encouraged and sanctioned by the ruling circles. The Czarist government endeavored to deflect popular anger over economic, political and military blunders by turning it against the Jews. This official policy found fertile ground in the deeply-rooted popular anti-Semitism of the Russian people. Hundreds of Jews lost their lives and thousands sustained injuries in the pogroms staged during that time. Thousands of Jewish homes and businesses were laid waste.

In 1905, an anti-Semitic booklet entitled *The Protocols of the Elders of Zion* was published in Russia. This potpourri of falsehoods, distortions and fabrications alleged the existence of a secret malevolent Jewish government working to impose Jewish domination over the whole world. The main thesis of this pamphlet, concocted by the Czarist secret police, drew on an ancient Christian fable and a host of 19th-century European publications which alleged the existence of a secret Jewish world council waging a war against Christendom by means of the most cruel and devious methods. Later editions of the *Protocols* included an appendix in which the "world-wide Jewish conspiracy" was linked with the First Zionist Congress convened in Basel in 1897 and with the name of Herzl. Translated into many languages and circulated in various countries, *The Protocols of the Elders of Zion,* became a classic work of anti-Semites the world over. Hitler, too, drew his inspiration from it.

The Dreyfuss trial and the pogroms in Russia were among the factors stimulating the rise of the Jewish national movement in Europe and the founding of the Zionist movement. Guided by the idea of return to the Land of Israel with the view of establishing a Jewish state there, it expressed the centuries-old Jewish longing for Zion. Zionism claimed to provide the solution to anti-Semitism and the predicament of the Jews which, it argued, could not be rectified in exile.

Despite its cultural advancements, the developments in Europe at the end of the 19th and early 20th centuries boded ill for the Jewish people. Anti-Semitism in its manifold guises grew in strength. World War I and its aftermath resulted in far-reaching political and social transformations. These changes, particularly in Germany, planted the seeds for the advent of reactionary forces culminating in Nazism, which were to inflict the greatest disaster on the Jewish people in its history — the Holocaust.

Nazis in Germany on the way to power

Political, economic and social conditions which evolved in Germany after World War I stimulated the reawakening of German nationalism and the founding of the Nazi party (National-Socialist German Workers' Party — *Nationalsozialistische Deutsche Arbeiterpartei* — NSDAP), headed by Adolf Hitler.

A descendant of a petty bourgeois Austrian family, Hitler lived in Vienna before World War I. In those years, Vienna, the capital of the Habsburg Empire, was the main scene of the national and social conflicts tearing at the fabric of the Austrian Empire. Hitler's ambition to become a great painter came to nought when his application to the Vienna Academy of Fine Arts was rejected. For the next few years he subsisted by selling his drawings. During those cheerless years Hitler consolidated his nationalist outlook which soon assumed the form of extreme anti-Semitism. Doubtless, it resulted in part from his frustration and failure to achieve his personal ambitions. With the outbreak of World War I, Hitler gave expression to his pan-German views by volunteering to serve in the German army. For the duration of the war he fought on the French front, advancing to the rank of lance-corporal. The news of the revolution in Germany, the abdication of the emperor, and the establishment of a republic there shocked him profoundly. He refused to resign himself to the situation; this was not what he had volunteered to fight for. Hitler stayed in the ranks and continued to serve in Munich where he met many officers and soldiers who opposed the socialist regime which had just been established in Bavaria. He worked in the Department of Propaganda and took an active part in local political life. While still in the army he attended meetings of the small Nazi party which had recently been organized in Munich. In April 1920 he resigned from the army to take over the reins of the Nazi party.

Hitler exploited the prevailing frustration and economic difficulties besetting Weimar Germany after World War I to gain mass support for his party. Demagoguery and anti-Semitism were his chief weapons. Hitler blamed the Jews for the German defeat in the war, claiming they were behind the November revolution of 1918 which "stabbed in the back" a successful army. According to Hitler, the Jews were responsible for the surrender on the front. He also held the Jews responsible for the harsh terms imposed on Germany by the Treaty of Versailles, as well as for the economic difficulties. The Weimar Republic, Hitler argued, was *de facto* ruled by Jews.

Racial theories served as the ideological cornerstone of the Nazi party from its inception. The first party manifesto published in 1920 provides ample evidence of the crucial role racism played in its world view. In his book *Mein Kampf* (My Struggle) written in 1923, Hitler elaborated extensively on the application of racial theories in politics, the economy, and particularly with regard to the Jews. According to him, civil rights should be granted only to members of the Aryan race. As a superior race, the Germans had the right to enslave and dominate other peoples. Since, so the argument went, human societies were engaged in a perpetual war for existence in which the strong prey on the weak, the use of force was a legitimate means to achieve that purpose. The German people was entitled to all the living space (*Lebensraum*) necessary for its existence and therefore it was justified in driving out other people living on these territories. This racist outlook provided the rationale for the Nazi ideology of expansion eastward (*Drang nach Osten*), i.e. the territories of Poland and the Soviet Union, their colonization by the Germans, and the enslavement of the Slavic peoples.

Hitler and the Nazis pushed these racial theories to their extremes as far as Jews were concerned. The Nazi outlook portrayed the Jews not just as an inferior race, but as subhumans, i.e. beyond the pale of the human race. Essentially the Jew was a dangerous virus infiltrating the body of the German people in order to achieve domination over it by enfeebling it from within. Jews tried to assimilate into German society and gain control over the centers of political and economic power, as well as over the mass media. Penetration of these centers of political power was accomplished, according to Hitler, by spreading the ideas of democracy, socialism and communism which the Jews disseminated in Germany itself as well as in other countries. These ideologies were held by Hitler as contradicting the natural order in the world. By destroying this order the Jews advanced toward the achievement of their objectives. Hitler believed in the existence of a world-wide Jewish conspiracy bent on ruling the whole world according to *The Protocols of the Elders of Zion*. He mentions this belief in *Mein Kampf*. The terror the unrestrained power of the Jews formed the foundation of Hitler's world view and exerted a profound influence on his thinking.

Half a million German Jews, the target of the most virulent anti-Semitic Nazi propaganda, were well integrated into German society. Assimilation was quite prevalent and some Jews even considered themselves Germans of Mosaic persuasion. The prevalence of German patriotism among them may be illustrated by the fact that in World War I, one hundred thousand German Jews served in the military and twelve thousand died at the front, fighting for the homeland. Hitler ascribed no significance to this whatsoever. He portrayed the devotion of German Jews to their country as an attempt to infiltrate the German nation in order to destroy it from within. Consequently he opposed assimilation and mixed marriages between Germans and Jews by which, he maintained, inferior Jewish blood intermixed with German blood and spoiled the superior qualities of the Aryan race. For the same reason he rejected extramarital relations between Jews and Germans.

Hitler viewed himself as a person whom Destiny and Providence had entrusted with the task of waging a relentless, uncompromising, life and death war against Jewry. He believed that a Jewish victory in this war would put an end to both the existence of Germany and the natural world order. By the same token, German victory would mean the liquidation of the Jewish virus and saving the world from chaos. By portraying the Jews as a virus, by his thorough dehumanization, Hitler paved the way for the physical extermination of the Jews. After all, the virus had to be annihilated.

In order to put into practice his political racist ideas, Hitler had first to take power in Germany. From the very beginning he viewed force as the sole means to achieve that purpose. The military arm of the Nazi party, the SA (*Sturmabteilung* — Storm Troops) was set up to fight the Socialists and Communists and as an instrument for gaining control over the state. Hitler's plans provided for exploiting the economic turmoil, rampant inflation, political instability and structural weakness of the Weimar Republic to achieve his objectives. More specifically, he planned to take power in Munich, the capital of Bavaria first, and use it as a launching pad for a march on Berlin. "The March on Berlin" was to be modelled after Mussolini's fascists' successful "March on Rome" in October 1922, as a result of which Mussolini was appointed dictator of Italy. Hitler regarded him as a model to be emulated. To increase his chances of success he recruited General Ludendorff, hoping the army would not dare to open fire on the marchers led by a widely-admired war hero.

The attempt to take over in Munich, in November 1923, later to be known as the "*Putsch*," ended in failure. The army remained loyal to the legal authorities; it opened fire on the marchers and suppressed the attempted coup by force. Hitler was arrested, tried and sentenced to five years in prison. He served only nine months, during which he wrote his book *Mein Kampf,* laying down in detail his ideological and political views.

Hitler learned the lesson of the failed *Putsch.* He realized that the legal means made available by the democratic system, and not violent takeover, would provide the instrument to achieve power. The inherent weakness of the Weimar democracy made recourse to legal means all the more attractive. At the same time, however, he reorganized and boosted the strength of the second instrument of his two-pronged assault — the military arm of the Nazi party. In 1925 he established the SS (*Schutzstaffel* —

6

6. A leaflet issued by the "Reichsbund Jüdischer Frontsoldaten" (Federal Association of Jewish Frontline Soldiers) in the early 1930s in Germany in response to mounting anti-Semitic propaganda. It appeals to German mothers, emphasizing the fact that twelve thousand Jewish soldiers died fighting for their homeland in World War I.

7. Jewish cemetery, Berlin. A plaque in honor of Jewish soldiers who fell in World War I.

8. Jewish cemetery, Berlin. Graves of Jewish soldiers who fell in World War I.

Defence Corps), a military formation which, despite its small size, was fiercely loyal and subordinated to him directly. He also set about reorganizing the SA as a mass formation which the Nazis could unleash in violent street clashes with Socialists and Communists.

Hitler's efforts to secure mass support for his party in the second half of the 1920s ended in failure. In the 1928 elections to the German parliament, the Reichstag, the NSDAP gained only 2.6% of the popular vote. Out of a total of 647 Reichstag deputies, the Nazis had just 12. In 1929 a world-wide economic crisis began which was to last several years. In Germany millions of people were unemployed and the country plunged into a period of social unrest. Scores of victims of clashes between the SA and Socialist and Communist demonstrators served to exacerbate the already difficult situation. In several consecutive elections in the years 1929–1932 the Nazi party progressively grew in strength. Hitler kept offering promises of peace and stability to the discontented German populace as well as the elimination of unemployment. In the July 1932 elections, the Nazis emerged with 230 Reichstag deputies and 37.3% of the vote. Despite the fact that Hitler had never gained an absolute majority of the vote, the President of Germany, Fieldmarshal Hindenburg, charged him with forming the government. On Janurary 30, 1933, Hitler was appointed as Chancellor of Germany. German conservative forces which had assisted Hitler in ascending to power hoped he would help them to suppress the Left. They also acted on the assumption that they would succeed in directing and controlling his actions to suit their own interests which in part diverged from and even contradicted Hitler's ideology. Their evaluation of Hitler and the Nazis proved to be woefully inadequate. Hitler used them in achieving his objective of taking power in Germany. The way toward implementing his policies, including those concerning the Jews, stood open.

9

9. The Munich Putsch (1923). Heinrich Himmler (fourth from left) with members of Hitler's Storm Troops (SA) behind the barricades in front of the War Ministry in Munich, November 9, 1923.

10. Fieldmarshal Hindenburg, President of Germany, receiving Hitler after his appointment as Chancellor of Germany.

11. Hitler attending the Nazi May Day Parade (1934).

12

13

12. Hitler at a mass meeting in 1934 (location unknown).

13. Hitler at a mass meeting of the Nazi party in the Grunewald stadium, Berlin, 1933.

14

15

14. Dr. Spiegel, a Jewish lawyer, being marched in Munich under SA escort; the sign he wears reads: "I shall never again complain to the police." He was later murdered in the Dachau concentration camp.

15. German judges taking the oath of loyalty to Hitler.

16

16. Prisoners' roll call at the Oranienburg concentration camp, which began operating on March 12, 1933.

17. The Reichstag ablaze, February 27, 1933.

17

18

18. SA guards at the entrance to a Jewish store on "Boycott Day." The sign says: "Germans beware! Do not buy from Jews."

PERSECUTION OF JEWS IN GERMANY 1939–1941

The economic boycott — April 1, 1933

With the appointment of Hitler as Chancellor of Germany, his anti-Semitic ideology became the official policy of the Reich toward its Jewish nationals. This policy was implemented in stages. In the first months after Hitler had taken office, the Nazis moved to take control of the power centers of the state. Hermann Goering, second in the Nazi hierarchy, was appointed Minister of Interior in Prussia, which enabled him to gain control of the police. The SS, under the command of Heinrich Himmler, and the SA were granted official status. The institutions which formed the mainstay of democracy such as parliament, political parties, trade unions, and the press were curtailed or dissolved altogether. Nazis were appointed to key positions in the state apparatus, replacing officials with liberal views. Mass arrests of Socialist, Communist and liberal activists were carried out, the detainees jailed or incarcerated in concentration camps set up for that purpose (the first such camp was established in Dachau in 1933). The administration of these camps was placed in the hands of the SA and SS who enjoyed complete freedom of action, unbound by the legal constraints which still applied in Germany. Terror, propaganda and provocation were the main instruments used by the Nazis to consolidate their power. Thus they exploited a fire set at the Reichstag building on February 27, 1933 to issue a series of emergency decrees suspending basic democratic freedoms, thereby paving the way for a totalitarian regime. Shortly thereafter, the Reichstag transferred its legislative authority to the government, i.e. to Hitler, who in effect became a dictator.

The arrests carried out in the first months of 1933 also swept up many Jews, although most of them were rounded up as activists of the political parties and organizations banned by the Nazis. The SA men expressed their joy and glee at the Nazi takeover by rioting and attacking Jews and Jewish institutions. During this stage, however, these acts were spontaneous and locally instigated.

The first comprehensive step taken by the Nazi leadership and the state against the Jewish community was the economic boycott declared on April 1, 1933. The Nazis justified the boycott as a reaction to "Jewish propaganda of atrocity and incitement directed against Germany from abroad." Jewish institutions in Germany were forced to issue messages denying the accusations against Germany published in other countries. The Nazi leadership issued instructions on the boycott saying, *inter alia*: "The boycott must hit the Jews where it hurts them most. A good German will no longer buy from the Jews." Parallel to preparations for an economic boycott, an extensive propaganda campaign was unleashed under the direction and inspiration of Josef Goebbels, Minister of Information and Propaganda of the Third Reich. Julius Streicher, a notorious Jew-hater and editor of the viciously anti-Semitic weekly *Der Stuermer,* was put in charge of organizing the boycott. Local action committees were set up throughout Germany to implement the boycott which was to affect Jewish businesses, merchandise, physicians and lawyers.

The anti-Jewish boycott to be staged throughout Germany was called for April 1, 1933. SS and SA guards were stationed in front of Jewish stores to warn Germans against patronizing them. On the same day mass meetings and demonstrations in support of the boycott were staged. Goebbels described boycott day in Berlin as follows: "I am touring the streets. . . . All Jewish stores are closed. SA men stand guard at the doors. The public has demonstrated its full solidarity everywhere. Discipline has been exemplary. An impressive spectacle! . . . In the afternoon 150,000 Berlin workers marched toward Lustgarten. . . . The boycott is a great moral victory for Germany."

When the boycott was announced its organizers did not reveal when it would end. But at midnight of the first day it was decided to discontinue it. Nazi Germany was still sensitive to negative reactions which the boycott and other forms of terror had aroused abroad. The official announcement said that "having achieved its purpose, the boycott has been ended." It is noteworthy that in a number of places only part of the German public complied with the boycott.

This operation marked the beginning of anti-Jewish measures initiated by the state. At this stage, Hitler and his government still preserved a "legal" framework for their anti-Jewish policies. The regime still took legal precautions by promulgating laws, regulations and decrees. However, in order to make sure that no Jew escaped the effects of their legislation, the Nazis had to define "who is a Jew" first. A relatively high incidence of mixed marriages in Germany necessitated a definition of the status of progeny of such marriages. To cope with this problem a decree defining a "non-Aryan" was promulgated on April 11, 1933. It said, *inter alia*: "A non-Aryan is anyone descended from non-Aryan, especially Jewish, parents or grandparents. One parent or grandparent classifies the descendant as non-Aryan. This is to be assumed especially if one parent or grandparent was of the Jewish faith."

By means of regulations and decrees, Jews were summarily dismissed or forcibly retired from the civil service, army, judiciary, institutions of higher learning, cultural institutions, and the press. Thousands of Jewish physicians were gradually forced from their positions. These mass dismissals left thousands of Jews with no source of livelihood, thereby undermining the economic existence of a broad section of the Jewish community.

19. The word "Jude" (Jew) and the Star of David on the window of a Jewish store, warning German customers not to patronize it. A common sight in Germany in the first months of 1933.

32

20

20. Burning of banned books on Berlin's Opera Square, May 10, 1933. A German-Jewish poet, Heinrich Heine, predicted over a hundred years ago: "Where books are burned, human beings are destined to be burned too."

On the night of May 10, 1933, a symbolic public ceremony of burning "harmful" books took place at the Opera Square in Berlin. The ceremony was organized by Goebbels who, in his capacity as Minister of Information and Propaganda, was in charge of the campaign of uprooting the Jews and their influence from German cultural life. The burning of "un-German" works was staged by an organization of Nazi students and it also took place in other university towns. Books disagreeable to Nazi ideology, especially those authored by Jews regardless of their content, were consigned to the flames. An index of banned books was drawn up and libraries were ordered to remove them from circulation. The censored works included books by Heinrich Heine, Thomas Mann, Sigmund Freud, Stefan Zweig and many others.

One hundred years before the Nazis put books to the torch, the great German poet of Jewish origin, Heine, said: "Wherever books are burned, people will also be burned."

21

22

21. Jews under SA escort forced to carry signs saying: "In response to the atrocity propaganda campaign, no German will buy from Jews."

22. Whoever buys from Jews is stealing the nation's assets" — inscription on a river boat.

23

25

24

23. "The Jews are our misfortune" inscription on an airplane fuselage.

24. An announcement posted in advance of "Boycott Day" calling on the German people not to buy from Jews, April, 1933.

25. SA men on "Boycott Day" with a sign saying: "Germans, do not buy from Jews!"

The Nuremberg Laws — September 1935

Anti-Jewish legislation reached its climax in the Nuremberg Laws. The name derives from the town of Nuremberg where the annual NSDAP congress formally adopted them on September 15, 1935. Two laws were promulgated: the "Reich Citizenship Law" and the "Law for the Protection of German Blood and Honor." The Citizenship Law stated, *inter alia*, that: "A Reich citizen is a subject of the state with German or cognate blood" and "a Reich citizen enjoys full political rights according to law." The second law included a number of provisions. First, marriages between Jews and persons of German or cognate blood were forbidden. Extramarital relations between these two groups were also forbidden. Jews were forbidden to employ female German domestic servants under forty-five years of age. Furthermore, Jews were forbidden to fly the German national colors. Instead they were allowed to display "Jewish colors." A supplementary regulation to the Reich Citizenship Law providing the basic definition of a Jew was promulgated on November 14, 1935. A Jew was anyone with at least three Jewish grandparents, or two Jewish grandparents, if he himself was of the Jewish faith or was married to a Jew. This regulation also defined a third category of "mixed offspring" (*Mischling*), i.e. persons who were neither Jews nor Aryans. This category comprised those with one or two Jewish grandparents. In the future these *Mischlinge* were to be subject to various discriminatory practices.

The Nuremberg Laws effectively repealed the civil equality granted to Jews by the Emancipation and transformed racism into a legal concept. Jews as individuals and as a community were set apart from Germans and deprived of fundamental civil liberties. Jewish children were removed from the German educational system or concentrated in separate classrooms. This operation was carried out ostentatiously and provocatively within the schools, where Jewish students were terrorized and humiliated without restraint.

The persecution of German Jews by isolating them socially and economically, as well as through anti-Jewish legislation, was meant to enable the Nazi rulers to realize one of their primary ambitions: to force the Jews to emigrate and to seize their property. At that time the political situation was not yet ripe for mass expulsions, so the Nazis did their utmost to make the Jews emigrate ostensibly of their own free will.

26

26. Front page of the anti-Semitic newspaper "Der Stürmer." The headline reads: "Jewish Murder Plan." Sub-heading: "The Jews are our misfortune."

27. Two Jewish pupils stand with bowed heads before their classmates. The inscription on the blackboard reads: "The Jew is our greatest enemy, beware of the Jew."

27

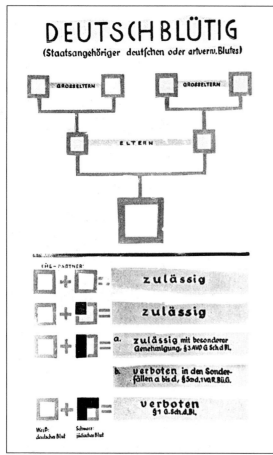

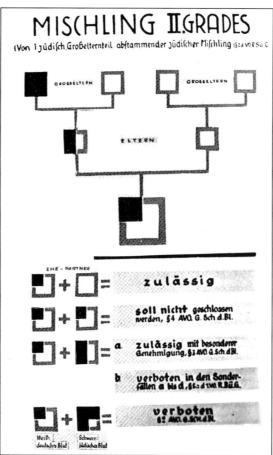

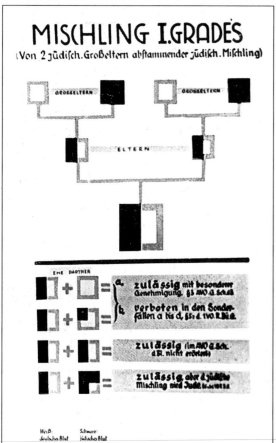

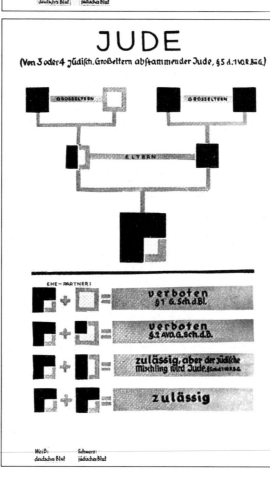

29

28. Illustration from the Nazi book "Rassenkunde und Bevölkerungspolitik," explaining the race laws introduced in 1935: a) pure-blooded German; b) mixed blood, second degree (one Jewish grandparent); c) mixed blood, first degree (two Jewish grandparents); d) full-blooded Jew.

29. Propaganda poster accusing the Jews of defiling the German race.

30. Nazi party rally in the Sports Palace in Berlin, August 15, 1935. The inscriptions read: "The Jews are our misfortune!" and "Women and girls! The Jews are your seducers!"

28

31

Reactions of German Jews

With Hitler's assumption of power, and particularly after the April 1 boycott, German Jews faced a new reality. They realized that difficult trials lay ahead. However, Jewish reactions to the new situation varied. Robert Weltsch, editor-in-chief of the Zionist newspaper *Juedische Rundschau* is remembered for his courageous response. On April 4, 1933, three days after the boycott, he published an article on the front page of his newspaper whose title "*Wear it with Pride, the Yellow Badge,*" became a watchword among German Jews. He said that the boycott should be turned into a day of Jewish reawakening and renewal. It also should mark the return to Jewry's fold of those who had become alienated from it. He argued that the mark of disgrace with which the Nazis sought to brand the Jews must be turned into an emblem of self-dignity. It must be noted, however, that Weltsch referred to the "Yellow Badge" in its symbolic meaning only; in 1933, German Jews were not yet required to wear this identifying sign, which was introduced in Germany only in 1941.

Some German Jewish leaders were gloomy concerning the future of Jews in that country. Rabbi Leo Baeck, a major figure among German Jewry, said that "the thousand year history of the German Jews has come to an end." Most Jews, however, simply lacked the foresight to envision the fate awaiting them. They hoped Hitler and Nazism amounted to yet another anti-Jewish outburst, the latest in the waves of anti-Semitism which had periodically swept the country. Although each such outbreak brought in its wake suffering and victims, German Jews had survived these ordeals and they would survive the present one, too. Many Jews also believed that by assuming the obligations of state power, including its relations with other countries, the Nazis would be compelled to discard the anti-Jewish plans formulated in their ideological manifestos when the party was in opposition. They saw the discontinuation of the April 1 boycott after just one day as an encouraging sign.

Prior to the Nazi rise to power, German Jews lacked a united body to represent its various communities, organizations and movements. With Hitler as Chancellor, it became clear that the new reality called for closing ranks and solving their internal differences if the deadly challenge was to be answered. In September 1933, an umbrella Jewish organization called "The Representation of German Jews" came into being with Rabbi Leo Baeck as its chairman. It united both Zionists and non-Zionists, orthodox Jews and assimilationists. Only a few marginal groups of German Jews remained outside this organization. Its main task was to represent German Jewry vis-à-vis the Nazi regime. Other tasks included expansion of the Jewish educational system, culture and sport, providing Jewish youth with vocational training as to enable them to engage in occupations still open to German Jews. Much thought was given to providing posssiblities for economic existence, welfare, religious activities, and training young people for building their future in the Land of Israel. It was a voluntary organization, lacking any official or legal status vis-à-vis the state, and its authority was not binding on the Jewish public.

32

31. A Jewish man and a Christian woman accused of intimate relations. The woman's sign reads: "I am the biggest pig around here because I make it only with Jews." The man's sign says: "I am a Jewboy who always takes German girls to my room." Hamburg, 1935.

32. "Wear it with Pride, the Yellow Badge" — title of an article in the Zionist newspaper "Jüdische Rundschau," April 4, 1933.

Despite the boycott, the anti-Jewish legislation, particularly the Nuremberg Laws, the ousting of thousands of Jews from government and public positions, their social isolation, the annulment of their citizenship or their becoming subjects of the state, many German Jews and their leaders still held fast to the hope that some form of coexistence with the Nazi regime could be worked out, even if they had to retain their inferior status. Their deep psychological attachments and cultural ties to Germany, together with their German patriotism, blinded many of the Jews to the realities facing them and to the course that the developments were taking. Their historical experience, rich as it was in memories of persecutions and oppression, could not warn them against the fate awaiting them.

It should be noted that in the periods between the assaults on their status and existence such as the boycott, the Nuremberg Laws and other measures, German Jews went through an interim period of relative calm which lasted several years. At that time Nazi Germany still displayed sensitivity to reactions abroad and sought to maintain economic ties with the external world which it needed to prepare itself for war in the future. The success of the Olympic Games scheduled to take place in Berlin in 1936 was an important consideration for Hitler who wanted to ward off an international boycott. He regarded massive international participation in the Games as bestowing legitimacy on him and his Nazi regime. This and other indications lulled some sections of the German Jewish community who continued to entertain illusions that some form of accommodation could still be reached.

Broadly speaking, in the years 1933–1938 German Jews moved to reorganize their communal structure to allow for some form of coexistence with the German society which had ejected them from its midst. Parallel with this effort, German Jewry undertook to train and prepare its young people for emigration, primarily to the Land of Israel. No matter how strong were the illusions concerning the plausibility of a continuing Jewish existence in Germany, they could not obscure the fact that the younger generation had no future in that country.

At that tragic period for German Jewry they provided an astonishing cultural efflorescence. Book publishing, theater, music and other spheres of cultural activity flourished within the framework of the Central Cultural Association ("Jüdischer Kulturverband").

33. Rabbi Joachim Prinz lecturing to Jewish youth in Berlin.

34. Hebrew classes for German Jews preparing to emigrate to Palestine.

35. Evening's entertainment by members of a Zionist youth movement in Germany in the early 1930s.

33

34

35

36

36. Jewish women athletes at a Maccabi championship meet in Berlin, 1935.

37. Bar-Kochba — Hakoah sports festival, Grunewald 1936.

38. Farewell party for a Youth Aliya group emigrating to Palestine. The sign reads: "The Land of Israel needs us — *we* need the Land of Israel."

39. Maccabi girl athletes at a sports competition, July 1934.

40. "Hahsharah" — agricultural training for Jewish youth preparing to emigrate to Palestine.

37

38

39

40

Emigration

There were several waves of emigration of Jews from Germany, each of them following in the wake of anti-Jewish measures taken by the Nazi regime. The first wave came shortly after the Nazi rise to power; within fifteen months some 50,000 Jews left the country. This number included Jews subject to arrest such as Liberals, Social Democrats and Communists. Some of them, having failed to find refuge abroad, had no choice but to return to Germany. Their return was motivated in part by the fact that the year 1934 was a relatively quiet one; it seemed that the situation had become stable and the trouble had passed.

A few thousand arrived in Eretz Israel despite the British ban on mass immigration there. In order to facilitate the absorption in Palestine of those Jews who managed to immigrate, an agreement was signed in 1933 between the Zionist Executive and the German authorities, known as the "Transfer Agreement." It provided for the indirect transfer to Palestine of part of the assets left behind by the emigrants. Efforts were also undertaken to organize the immigration of youth as part of the *Youth Aliyah* program; thousands of young people came to Palestine in this way. At that time the *Hehalutz* movement in Germany encompassed thousands of young people who had undergone agricultural and vocational retraining to prepare them for work in the Land of Israel.

The second wave of emigration followed in the aftermath of the Nuremberg Laws. These enactments made it clear to German Jews that their situation was deteriorating and that emigration was their only choice. Altogether in the years 1933–1935, some 78,000 Jews left Germany. By November 1938, this number had reached 150,000 — about 30% of the total German Jewish population.

42

43

41. Jews queuing in front of Lloyd's travel agency in Berlin to obtain entry visas to countries of refuge.

42. On board the ship "St. Louis," which sailed for Cuba from Hamburg in 1939.

43. Jews boarding a ship leaving Germany.

44. Jews in Berlin registering for emigration to Palestine.

45. Jews attempting illegal border crossing to Switzerland.

41

Military expansion

In 1935 Hitler felt that his power in Germany and his position abroad were consolidated enough to enable him to embark on a course of military expansion. He was reassured by the lack of response on the part of the victorious World War I powers to the reinstitution of compulsory military service in Germany and the beginning of open rearmament of the German army in violation of the Treaty of Versailles. He construed that lack of response and willingness to compromise as weakness. In his view, the time was ripe for implementing a policy of expansion. On January 13, 1935, the Germans annexed the Saargebiet. On March 7, 1936, German troops entered the demilitarized zone in the Rhineland, thus violating the Locarno Treaty of 1925 signed between Germany, on the one hand, and France and Belgium, on the other. The lack of response by the Western countries to this step, together with the well-attended opening of the Olympic Games in Berlin, further strengthened Hitler's position within Germany and encouraged him to carry on with his expansionist policies. In 1936, an axis was forged between Germany and Fascist Italy, later to be joined by Japan. In the same year General Franco led a Fascist revolt in Spain. Germany and Italy sent arms and troops to assist Franco against the legal Republican regime. On March 12, 1938, the German army entered Austria, which became part of the Third Reich. Two days later, Hitler was enthusiastically received in Vienna. In a plebiscite held one month

47

46. German army entering the Saargebiet, January 13, 1935.

47. German army entering Austria, March 12, 1938.

48. A poster calling on Austrians to support the annexation of their country by Germany.

49. Austrian crowds (at the Hofburg in Vienna) cheering the Germans entering their country.

46

48

51

52

after the entry of German troops, 99.75% of Austrians voted in favor of *Anschluss* — union of Austria with Germany. The fate of 200,000 Austrian Jews, most of whom lived in Vienna, was thus sealed.

After Austria came the turn of Czechoslovakia. Hitler issued a demand that the Sudetenland, an area on the border between Czechoslovakia and Germany inhabited mostly by Germans, be annexed to the Reich. On September 29, 1938, British Prime Minister Neville Chamberlain, French Premier Edouard Daladier, Mussolini and Hitler met in Munich. At what was to be called the "Munich Pact," Chamberlain and Daladier abandoned their Czechoslovak ally and acquiesced to Hitler's demands by giving their consent to the annexation of the Sudetenland to Germany over the objections of the government of Czechoslovakia. Chamberlain returned triumphantly to London, announcing he had succeeded in preserving world peace.

Having annexed the Sudetenland, Hitler declared that he entertained no further territorial ambitions, but on March 15, 1939, Nazi troops overran Czechoslovakia without resistance. Slovakia became "independent," i.e. a puppet state of Nazi Germany. Bohemia became the Protectorate of Bohemia and Moravia, ruled *de facto* by Germany. Carpathian Ukraine which had formed part of Czechoslovakia was ceded to Hungary, Hitler's ally. Over 350,000 Jews in Czechoslovakia found themselves under the direct rule of the Nazis or their allies. After swallowing Czechoslovakia, Hitler annexed the Lithuanian port city of Klaipeda, which the Germans called Memel.

50. Viennese Jews forced to scrub the city pavements, March, 1938.

51. Poster proclaiming: "When Jewish blood drips from the knife . . ."

52. "Jude" (Jew) painted on the entrance to a Jewish store in Austria.

53 Hitler and Chamberlain at the Munich conference, which sealed Czechoslovakia's fate.

54. German troops entering Prague.

The year 1938 — radicalization of anti-Jewish policy

In 1938 Nazi anti-Jewish policy underwent a far-reaching radicalization as it became increasingly violent. Within a few months all anti-Jewish decrees and regulations which had been promulgated over the previous five years in Germany were applied summarily against the Austrian Jews who had become subjects of the Reich. Jews were rounded up and terrorized; scores were dispatched to concentration camps. Adolf Eichmann, the Gestapo specialist for Jewish affairs, arrived in Vienna to expedite Jewish emigration. He set up an Emigration Office there charged with speeding up forcible emigration of Jews from Austria.

The removal of Jews from German economic life shifted into higher gear. The transfer of Jewish property and businesses to Aryans, the so-called "Aryanization" policy which until then had been ostensibly carried out voluntarily, became obligatory. From April to December 1938, decrees were promulgated ordering the liquidation of Jewish businesses and their transfer to Aryans. These decrees effectively and finally removed the Jews from economic life, leaving them without livelihood. The compensation offered to them amounted to a miniscule percentage of their property, valued at 7 billion marks. Additional anti-Jewish decrees issued in 1938 included the following:

— Jews whose first names were not identifiably Jewish were required to add "Israel" (men) and "Sarah" (women) to their names.
— All Jews over the age of 15 were required to carry an identity card.
— Passports of Jews were stamped with the letter J (*Jude*). This requirement came, to no small extent, as the result of a request by the Swiss government which sought to restrict the immigration of German Jews into its country.
— Jews were required to live in separate buildings.
— The legal status of the Jewish community was abolished.

The Nazi authorities supplemented these measures by setting up a representative Jewish body, a Judenrat of sorts for all German Jews, named the "Union of the Jews in Germany." Membership in the Union was obligatory for every person defined as a Jew by the Nuremberg Laws. The establishment of this organization brought to an end the activity of the voluntary Jewish body, the Representation of the Jews in Germany. Working in new and exceptionally difficult conditions, the Union endeavored to ease the situation of German Jews as much as possible under the circumstances.

In 1938 intense pressure was applied to force Jews to leave Germany. Several thousand Jews were rounded up under various shallow pretences and incarcerated in the concentration camps of Dachau, Buchenwald and Mauthausen; they could buy their freedom only by emigrating from the country. However, they had nowhere to go. The British government closed Palestine almost completely to Jewish immigration; other countries too kept their gates shut. On October 28, 1938, some 17,000 Jews of Polish nationality were arrested in Germany. Several weeks previously the Polish government had annuled their citizenship. These stateless Jews were expelled to Polish territory, but the Polish government refused them entry. The deportees were kept in an

55. Herszel Grynszpan, a Jewish youth who shot and fatally wounded the third secretary of the German Embassy in Paris to avenge the deportation of his parents to Zbaszyn, Poland, in October 1938. The Germans seized upon this act as a pretext for unleashing the violence of "Kristallnacht" (The Night of Broken Glass), November 9–10, 1938.

open field in no-man's land near the Polish town of Zbaszyn. Polish Jews and the Joint Distribution Committee (JDC) came to their aid. Finally after several months and following intense lobbying by Jewish organizations, the Polish government agreed to let them in.

Among the deportees in Zbaszyn were the parents of a 17-year-old Jewish youth, Hershel Grynszpan, who then lived in Paris. Unsettled by the news that his parents were among the deportees, he went to the German embassy in Paris on November 7, 1938 and shot the first German official he met. Ernst von Rath, a third secretary at the embassy, was wounded and later died.

The Nazis had long been planning for an organized pogrom against the Jews and this incident provided the opportune moment. Goebbels called the signals for the pogrom, later to be known as *Kristallnacht* (Night of Broken Glass), which took place on the night of November 9–10, 1938. About 1400 synagogues and prayer rooms were burned or destroyed. Windows of Jewish apartments, offices, stores, schools and institutions all over Germany were shattered. Some of them were looted and laid waste. Streets were littered with shards of broken glass (thus the name of the pogrom). Over 30,000 Jewish men, mostly from the free professions, were rounded up and placed in concentration camps. More than 300 Jews were murdered and many more wounded. Vienna did not lag behind German cities: 42 synagogues were destroyed and 7,800 Jews were arrested. One German report on the event mentions 680 cases of suicide among German Jews in the aftermath of the *Kristallnacht.*

On November 12, 1938, a meeting attended by Heydrich took place at Goering's office. During that meeting it was decided to impose a fine of one billion marks on the Jews and to compel them to repair the damages. Insurance companies were required to pay compensation for damages to the state coffers instead of to the Jewish victims.

In the aftermath of *Kristallnacht,* the flow of Jewish emigration from Germany intensified. The Jews no longer entertained any illusions as to their future in that country. The only obstacle was the shortage of places of asylum. The story of the vessel "St. Louis" is a good example. In May 1939, "St. Louis" left Hamburg harbor with 900 Jews on board. Despite the fact that the passengers had entry visas to Cuba, the local authorities prevented them from disembarking. The United States, too, refused them entry as did other American countries. After many ordeals the ship sailed back to Europe. Its passengers shared the fate of other European Jews in the Holocaust.

The Nazis did all they could to step up the forced emigration of Jews from Germany. On January 24, 1939 Goering issued a directive which opened with the words: "All measures must be taken for the stepped-up emigration of Jews from Germany." It also spoke about the need to establish "a central Reich organization for emigration of Jews from Germany" to be headed by Heydrich. Adolf Eichmann, who had done an excellent job in organizing the forcible exit of Jews from Austria, was entrusted with the same task in Prague and Berlin. Throughout 1939, in the aftermath

56. The Oranienburgerstrasse synagogue in Berlin consumed by fire on Kristallnacht.

57. The interior of the Fasanenstrasse synagogue in Berlin after its destruction on Kristallnacht.

58. The Fasanenstrasse synagogue in Berlin before being torched.

59. Burning dome of the Fasanenstrasse synagogoue.

56

57

58

59

of *Kristallnacht,* 78,000 Jews left the old Reich — the largest number to leave in one year. Altogether some 300,000 Jews left the country up to the outbreak of World War II. Some 110,000 Austrian Jews, over half of its Jewish population, left as well. Anti-Jewish policies similar to those applied in Germany were implemented in the Protectorate of Bohemia and Moravia. Before the outbreak of the war, 25,000 Jews left Czechoslovakia. Jewish emigration from Germany continued even during the first two years of the war, although on a smaller scale, until October 1941 when it was officially forbidden.

In a speech delivered in the Reichstag on January 30, 1939, more than eight weeks after *Kristallnacht,* Hitler said: "... Today I will be a prophet again: If international finance Jewry within Europe and abroad should succeed once more in plunging the peoples into a world war, then the consequence will be not the Bolshevization of the world and therewith a victory of Jewry, but on the contrary, the destruction of the Jewish race in Europe."

World War II which broke out seven months after this speech provided Hitler with the opportunity to carry out his plans for the destruction of the Jews.

60

60. Smashed window of a Jewish store after Kristallnacht.

61. Burning synagogue in Baden-Baden, Germany.

62. Baden-Baden synagogue before Kristallnacht.

61

62

BADEN-BADEN Synagoge

63

64

58

65

63. Synagogue in Siegen, Germany,
during Kristallnacht.

64. Synagogue in Siegen, Germany,
during Kristallnacht.

65. The synagogue in Worms, Germany,
on the morning of November 10, 1938.

68

66. Registration of prisoners in Dachau concentration camp.

67, 68. Jews in Baden-Baden on their way to a concentration camp.

69. Deportation of Jews from Klaipeda
(Memel), annexed by Germany from
Lithuania in March, 1939.

EUROPEAN JEWS UNDER NAZI RULE AND TERROR 1939-1941

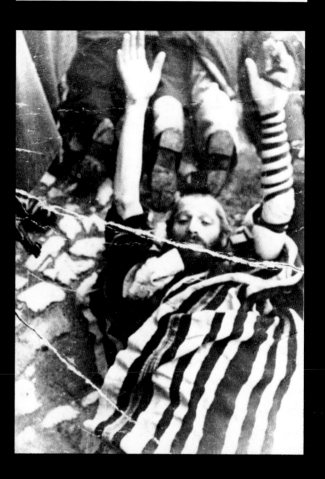

DIVISION OF POLAND
BETWEEN GERMANY AND U.S.S.R.
Agreement Signed on August 23, 1939

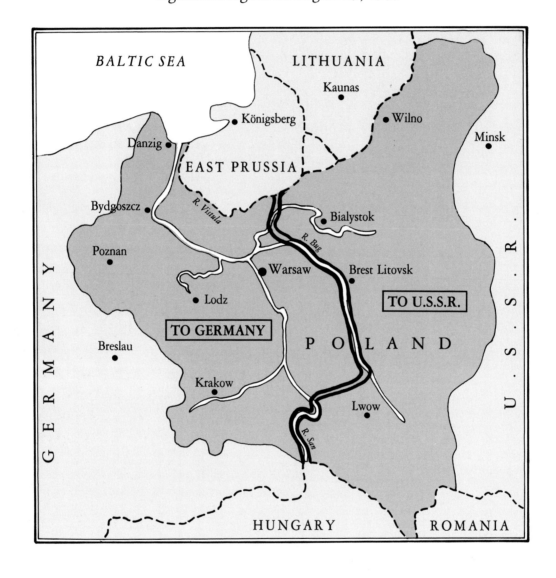

EUROPEAN JEWS UNDER NAZI RULE AND TERROR 1939–1941

The occupation of Poland

At dawn on September 1, 1939 the German army invaded Poland. World War II began. One week previously, on August 23, 1939, a non-aggression agreement known as the Ribbentrop-Molotov Pact had been signed between Germany and the Soviet Union. In a secret protocol to this pact, the two signatories divided Poland and defined their spheres of influence in Eastern Europe. This agreement concluded between two fierce ideological foes served the expansionist interests of both countries. Germany was given the guarantee that its attack on Poland, far from encountering Soviet resistance, would actually be aided by the Soviet conquest of Eastern Poland. Furthermore, in the event of England and France coming to the aid of their Polish ally, the Germans, having protected their eastern flank, would be able to fight on one front only in the West. For its part, the Soviet Union was given a free hand to annex large areas of Eastern Poland as well as to expand its domination and sphere of influence in the Baltic countries.

The war against Poland lasted less than four weeks. Western and Central Poland were quickly overrun by the German army. The Red Army, acting in accordance with the provisions of the Ribbentrop-Molotov Pact, entered Eastern Poland on September 17, 1939, and occupied Western Byelorussia and Western Ukraine.

The parts of Poland occupied by Nazi Germany were removed from the military administration, placed under the authority of other state agencies, and divided into two parts. One area comprising Western and Northern Poland, including the second largest Polish city of Lodz, were incorporated into the Third Reich. Some 600,000 Jews lived there. Southern-Central Poland, including the cities of Warsaw, Krakow and Lublin, were not annexed by the Reich. Instead they became a separate administrative–territorial entity called the General Government. Some 1,400,000 Jews resided in this area. Altogether, out of a total of 3.35 million Polish Jews, over two million found themselves under German rule, with the remaining 1.3 million living in areas annexed by the Soviet Union. Over 250,000 Jews escaped from the areas overrun by the Nazis to the Soviet occupied zone. Some of them fled during the fighting. Others made their way eastward until the winter of 1939–40 when the new German–Soviet border was still passable. Afterward, crossing the border posed a difficult and complicated task due to reinforced defences and guards. In October 1939, the city of Vilna, where a large Jewish concentration was to be found, was ceded by the Soviets, who had annexed it earlier, to the Lithuanian Republic. Jewish refugees from the Polish territories annexed by the Soviet Union started flowing to the city. They included large numbers of members of Zionist youth movements, yeshiva students and others who hoped they would be able to make their way to Palestine or to free western countries. By the end of 1939 some 15,000 Jewish refugees had arrived in Vilna across the new Lithuanian–Soviet border. Thousands of them succeeded in leaving Lithuania to Palestine and some European countries, with the help of the Japanese consul in Kovno, Sempo Sugihara.

70. Ribbentrop and Molotov signing the German-Soviet Non-Aggression Pact in Moscow, August 23, 1939.

71. German soldiers removing a Polish border-post barrier.

70

Military campaigns and political developments in Europe

From September 1939 until the spring of 1940, a period of relative calm set in on the warfront in Western Europe along the Franco–German border. The French, well-entrenched in the fortifications of the Maginot line, faced the Germans poised along the strongholds of the Siegfried line. This short lull came to an end when Germany launched its offensive in Western Europe by attacking neutral countries without warning. On April 9, 1940, they overran Denmark without resistance and invaded Norway. Due to the intervention of British troops in the fighting, the conquest of Norway took three months. On May 10, they invaded Holland, Belgium and Luxemburg — all of them neutral countries — thus bypassing the Maginot line from the north. Holland and Belgium were used as a corridor for the invasion of France. The rapid destruction of French military forces followed. France collapsed and surrendered on June 22, 1940. The bulk of the British Expeditionary Force operating in France was evacuated to England from the French port of Dunkirk. Northern and Western France, including Paris, were occupied by the Germans. Southern France retained a degree of independence under the Vichy government headed by Marshal Pétain, which collaborated with the Germans. The French general de Gaulle crossed over to Britain where he continued to call on the French people to carry on the struggle against the Germans. On June 10, 1940, before the surrender of France, Fascist Italy joined Germany by declaring war against Britain and France.

As territorial and political developments were reconstituting the map of Western and Northern Europe, events in the East also took their course. In the middle of June 1940, the Soviet Union seized the Baltic countries of Lithuania, Latvia and Estonia without resistance, turning them into Soviet republics. At the end of June, Romania gave in to a Soviet ultimatum and ceded it Bessarabia and Northern Bukovina. Under

72. German planes bombing Athens.

73. German troops marching under the Arc de Triomphe in Paris, July, 1940.

74. Rotterdam, Holland, in the wake of German air-raids, Mary, 1940.

German and Italian pressure, Romania was also forced to cede Northern Transylvania to Hungary. By late November 1940, Romania and Hungary joined the Axis, thereby allying themselves with Nazi Germany. In April 1941, the German army invaded Yugoslavia and moved against Greece. Soon both these countries were occupied jointly by Germany and Italy. In part of Yugoslavia, the ostensibly independent puppet state of Croatia came into being. Bulgaria, a German ally, annexed parts of Yugoslavia and Greece. By spring 1941, all of Europe with the exception of the Soviet Union, Britain, Ireland, Spain, Portugal, Switzerland and Sweden had been occupied either by Nazi Germany or one of its allies.

The persecution of Jews in the territories of Western Europe occupied by the Nazis commenced soon thereafter. There were some 350,000 Jews in France, 90,000 in Belgium, 140,000 in Holland, 3,500 in Luxemburg, 8,000 in Denmark, and 2,000 in Norway. The Nazis applied all their customary measures against the Jewish populations of these countries: enforcement of the Nuremberg Laws with their definition of a Jew, expropriation and plunder of Jewish property, and its transfer to Aryans. Jews were barred from a broad range of free professions. About 20,000 Jews from Alsace-Lorraine which had been wrested from France and annexed to Germany, together with thousands of Jews from the Franco–German border areas, were expelled to unoccupied France. In France itself the first victims were scores of thousands of Jews lacking French citizenship, mostly refugees who had arrived there in the 1930s. The Vichy government interned them in detention camps. However, the anti-Jewish measures taken during the first years of German occupation in Western Europe were not as draconian as those applied in occupied Poland. In Southern Europe, where 75,000 Jews lived in Yugoslavia and 77,000 in Greece, anti-Jewish decrees and other measures were put into effect without delay.

In July 1940, after the surrender of France, top Nazi officials put forward a plan to deport all European Jews to the island of Madagascar, a French colony off the coast of Eastern Africa. The prevailing feeling in Germany was that the war would soon be won and as part of a peace treaty with France, Madagascar could be designated as the site of a huge ghetto for all European Jews. It is noteworthy that the plan to transfer the Jews to Madagascar had not originated in Germany. As early as 1937 the Polish government had dispatched a mission to the island to examine the possibility of resettling Polish Jews there. At any rate, the German "Madagascar plan" remained on paper only, as Germany did not gain control of the island. Political and military developments in Europe soon opened other opportunities for the Nazis to solve the Jewish question.

Thus it came about that by the spring of 1941, the overwhelming majority of European Jews found themselves under the rule of Germany and its allies. They were headed toward unprecedented catastrophe.

73

74

Persecution of the Jews

The occupation of Poland marked a new, much more violent stage in German policy toward the Jews. Thousands of Jews had already been killed in fighting and during air raids on Polish cities. Scores of others were murdered in pogroms perpetrated by German soldiers, particularly the SS and the *Einsatzgruppen* (the notorious special-duty detachments of the SS. Subordinated to Heydrich himself, they were set up in advance of the invasion of Poland for the purpose of policing the occupied areas and carrying out measures against the Jews). German soldiers would seize Jews on the streets, tear or hack off their beards and sidelocks, and terrorize them in various ways.

On September 21, 1939, when the fighting in Poland was still raging, Heydrich issued an "urgent letter" (*Schnellbrief*) of instructions for the *Einsatzgruppen* concerning the treatment of Jews in the occupied territories. In the first section Heydrich emphasized that as far as anti-Jewish policy was concerned, a distinction must be made between the "final goal" (*Endziel*), on which he failed to elaborate, and the "stages leading to the fulfillment of this final goal," which he listed in detail. These stages comprised measures which were to be activated immediately. They included ejection of Jews from villages and towns to larger cities where they would be concentrated in ghettos located at railroad junctions or along railroad lines. The reference to "railroad lines" intimated that ghettoization would be temporary and that trains would serve as a means of transporting the Jews to other destinations, possibly that "final goal" which Heydrich had mentioned earlier. It is doubtful whether as early as September 1939, Heydrich knew exactly what this "final goal" amounted to, but even then it must have entailed something far more drastic than the ghettoization of Jews in occupied Poland. In any event, in the same set of instructions Heydrich ordered a census of the Jewish population and the establishment of "Councils of Jewish Elders" (later known as Judenräte), comprised of rabbis and other communal leaders. The Judenräte were charged with managing the ghettos after they were established, and their members were responsible with their lives for implementing German directives to the letter.

Anti-Jewish measures in Poland were promulgated in a rapid succession of decrees issued at the onset of the occupation. Jews over the age of 10 were ordered to wear an identifying mark in the form of a patch or a yellow Star of David on the front and back of outer garments. In the General Government, a white armband with a blue Star of David was instituted. Jews were banned from using public transport, using sidewalks, entering public places, transacting business in stores and markets during busy hours, and subjected to a host of other restrictive measures.

The concentration of the Jewish population in ghettos involved the deportation and transfer of hundreds of thousands of people from one place to another. Tens of thousands of Jews were expelled into the General Government from the Polish territories annexed to the Reich, particularly from the Lodz area (renamed Wartegau by the Germans), with the aim of making the Reich *Judenrein* (cleansed of Jews). Within the General Government itself, Jews were ejected from small towns and moved into larger cities. Collective punishments were imposed against them and "collective responsibility" instituted. This meant that for an offence committed by an individual, the whole group

75

75. German soldiers on their way to
Poland. The inscription on the railway car
reads: "We are going to Poland to strike
at the Jews."

or community was punished. Already during the first months of the occupation, dozens of Jews were executed for real or fictitious offences that just one person was accused of committing.

The Nazis regarded the Judenräte as an instrument for the implementation of their anti-Jewish policies. They used them as conduits for transmitting their orders and, at the same time, coerced them into carrying them out. Punishments were meted out to members of the Judenräte, many of whom paid with their lives for not complying with the German orders. For their part, the Judenräte sought in every way possible to soften the German measures and make the lives of the ghetto residents somewhat more tolerable. However their power and the means at their disposal were extremely limited. Although the Judenräte were established by German orders, circumstances turned them into the only existing form of Jewish leadership which had to act during a period of unprecedented suffering as the successor to the traditional Jewish community — the *kehillah*.

Prior to the ghettoization of Jews and in the course of their incarceration in the ghettos, they were stripped of their property and deprived of their sources of livelihood. Real estate owned by Jews was seized as part of the "Aryanization" campaign or transferred to special Trusteeship Bureaus. Their bank accounts were frozen and they were forbidden to keep more than 2,000 zlotys in cash — a negligible amount in those times. In addition, the Germans imposed so-called "contributions" (collective levies) amounting to millions of zlotys in cash, gold and other valuables. The collection of these contributions fell within the responsibilities of the Judenräte. These policies left the Jews destitute, exposed to hunger and cold.

76

76, 77. Maltreatment of Jews in Poland. Jews were compelled to sit for hours with their hands behind their heads while soldiers and civilians looked on (locations unknown).

78. Brutalizing of Jews in Poland
(location unknown).

80

79. A rabbi in Lodz forced to carry a sign reading: "We wanted war." The inscription on the garbage cart says: "The Jews are our misfortune." Jews surrounding the cart were forced to carry brooms.

80. A group of Jews being forced to sing hassidic songs in Szczebrzeszyn, Poland.

81

82

81, 82. SS men "amusing" themselves by cutting off the beard of a Jew in Plock, Poland.

83, 84. Slovak collaborators maltreating Jews.

83

84

85

85. Maltreatment of Jews in Poland.
Jews being forced to clown for the
amusement of the local population.

86

86. A Jew being forced to wrap himself
in his prayer shawl before execution in
Tarnow, Poland.

87. Massacre of Jews in Žarki, Poland. A
Jew wearing his prayer shawl and
phylacteries recites Kaddish over bodies
of Jews murdered by the Germans.

88

88. "Black Sabbath" in Salonika, Greece,
July 11, 1942. Some ten thousand
Jewish men were assembled.

89

89. Amsterdam. Round-up of young
Jews, February 22, 1941.

90

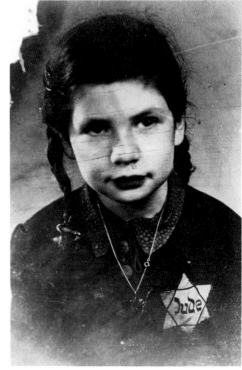

92

90. Jewish boys with the Yellow Badge on their backs in Minsk, Soviet Union.

91. Jewish boys with large Stars of David on their shirts.

92. Young Jewish girl from Germany.

91

93. Old Jew in the ghetto wearing the Star of David.

94. A woman vendor selling Star of David armbands in the Warsaw ghetto.

Forced labor

Already in the first days of the occupation, German soldiers began seizing Jews from streets and homes and putting them to work in clearing rubble, repairing roads, sweeping streets and buildings, and other jobs. On October 26, 1939 the General Government administration issued a decree on forced labor duty for all Jews aged 14 to 60. The Judenräte were required to supply quotas of forced labor workers as needed by the Germans. Often the Jewish workers would return home after a day's work only to be summoned to report for the same work the next day. Many of them were taken away to remote work places for weeks, even months at a time. Brutal treatment, beatings, insults and humiliations were the daily fare of Jewish workers employed at backbreaking labor from dawn to dusk regardless of weather conditions.

Thousands upon thousands of Jews were sent from the ghettos to forced labor camps which had been set up throughout Poland. Most of these camps were concentrated in the Lublin district where Jews worked at the construction of fortifications on the new border with the Soviet Union, road and bridge construction, draining marshes, etc. Terrible living conditions, substandard nutrition, lack of medical assistance, and excruciating labor made life in the camps unbearable. Mortality was endemic. Many of the workers returned to the ghettos with illnesses and disabilities they had contracted in the camps. Jewish skilled workers were recruited into forced labor in large factories and workshops where working conditions were somewhat superior to those prevailing elsewhere in the forced labor market. In certain places Jews even received wages, though far lower than those paid to Poles doing the same work.

German firms took advantage of cheap Jewish labor by setting up workshops in the ghettos for dressmaking, carpentry, and the manufacture of brushes, furs, etc. The Judenräte set up their own workshops to provide employment to ghetto residents and to prove to the German authorities that the ghetto was a productive economic factor contributing to the war effort. As the war continued, the German demand for labor grew, thereby encouraging the hope that the ghetto's ability to demonstrate its economic indispensability would more effectively assure its continued existence. On their part, both the German authorities in charge of the ghetto system and German firms benefited from the ghetto workshops by selling their cheaply-acquired output at a high profit. Ghetto residents succeeded in smuggling out part of the products manufactured by their workshops to pay for food, which was then smuggled back in. In this way they strove to combat hunger in the ghetto.

95. Forced labor in Cracow, Poland. Jews sweeping the city streets.

96. Forced labor in Cracow, Poland.

97

98

100. Forced labor in the Lodz area.

101. Children on their way to forced labor.

102. Jews being assembled for forced labor.

THE GHETTOS

103. Crowded street in the Warsaw ghetto.

THE GHETTOS

Usually the oldest and most rundown city districts previously inhabited by Jews were designated as ghetto sites. The Jews were told to move into the ghetto on very short notice — sometimes one day and in some cases even within a few hours. Usually the Judenrat was charged by the local German authorities with effecting the transfer to the ghetto. In certain places Jews were allowed to take with them only hand luggage. On occasion the Judenrat was given permission to hire carts from local residents to convey belongings to the ghetto.

The first ghetto was set up as early as October 1939 in the town of Piotrkow Trybunalski. Shortly thereafter a huge ghetto with 160,000 Jewish residents was formed in Lodz. Ghettoization of Jews in all large Polish cities quickly followed. The Warsaw ghetto, sealed in October 1940, was the largest with a population of 450,000 to 500,000, which also included Jews brought from the surrounding towns and villages. Leaving the ghetto without a permit issued by the German authorities was punishable by death.

The Judenräte were charged with the administration of ghetto life. A Jewish police force subordinated to the Judenrat was set up to maintain public order within the ghetto. Its policemen were armed only with sticks. On occasion it resorted to violent means to perform its tasks and even put people in jails set up in the ghettos. The methods and conduct of the Jewish policemen often aroused the criticism and animosity of ghetto residents. At the same time, however, there were many policemen who did their utmost to aid their suffering brethren by smuggling in food, enabling them to leave the ghetto, etc.

Ghetto residents lived in terrible congestion. In some ghettos two or three families composed of eight to ten persons each lived in one room. In the Warsaw ghetto, for example, one-third of the city's population, not counting Jews from district towns, was compressed into 4.5% of the city area. Inhuman sanitary conditions practically ruled out even a minimal level of personal hygiene. Illnesses and epidemics inevitably followed, taking an ordinately high toll of victims among ghetto residents.

Ghettoization was also crucial to the implementation of other German plans in the occupied Polish lands. One of those plans provided for the deportation of Jews from Germany, Austria and Czechoslovakia to the Nisko district in the southeastern part of the General Government. According to another plan, a Jewish "Reservat" from these countries was to be established in the Lublin area. In fact, thousands of Jews were deported there in the fall and winter of 1939–40, but due to organizational difficulties and the opposition of Governor Frank of the General Government, who wanted to control the deportation, these plans failed to be implemented.

Coping with hunger and disease

An implicit objective which the Germans sought to achieve by ghettoization was to starve the Jewish population to death. Hunger afflicted the ghetto residents more than any other hardship. The food ration per person in the Warsaw ghetto consisted of 180 grams of bread a day, 220 grams of sugar a month, and several other products in miniscule amounts. It amounted to a hunger ration which offered no possibility of sustenance. The situation in the other ghettos was similar and in some ghettos no food was supplied at all. The combination of hunger, indescribable congestion and lack of basic sanitation inevitably resulted in disease such as typhoid epidemics and resultant high rates of mortality.

Ghetto residents coped with hunger through all available means. The most prevalent was smuggling food into the ghetto. Many engaged in this trade including children, whose quickness and agility served them well in sneaking out to the "Aryan side" to smuggle food into the ghetto. Substantial quantities of food reached the ghetto via this route. However, only the wealthy few could afford to buy food on the black market. Most ghetto residents, particularly those from elsewhere and refugees who had arrived destitute, lacked money or valuables to purchase smuggled food. Various ghetto institutions, organizations and the Judenräte set up soup kitchens where the needy could have a bowl of warm soup, sometimes with bread, for free or for a token fee. In a number of ghettos, particularly the smaller ones, hunger and mass mortality were staved off. However, in larger ghettos, mainly in Warsaw, thousands upon thousands died of starvation. In 1941, over several months, five thousand people a month died of hunger. It was primarily children who succumbed to starvation and disease.

Medical services in the ghetto were overwhelmed by the task of combating disease and epidemics. A lack of medicines, isolation wards and hospital rooms was part of the ghetto reality. Superhuman efforts by doctors and nurses in preventive medicine, in maintaining a minimum standard of cleanliness, and in combating the diseases themselves could not prevent the spread of epidemics. Furthermore, the existence of contagious diseases in the ghetto, even the existence of hospital wards, had to be concealed from the Germans. The Nazis did not hesitate to execute patients, allegedly to prevent the spread of disease outside the ghetto. At a later stage the

104. Jews from Kutno, Poland, on their way to the ghetto.

105. Jews from Warsaw, Poland, on their way to the ghetto.

106. Jews from Kutno, Poland, on their way to the ghetto.

107. Jews from Cracow, Poland, on their way to the ghetto.

Germans prohibited childbirth in the ghetto, the offenders being threatened with death. For this reason, infants, whose numbers were in any case very limited due to the appalling conditions of the ghetto life, were delivered clandestinely by Jewish doctors and nurses.

Nearly all ghetto residents engaged in the struggle against hunger and disease. In the Warsaw ghetto "tenement committees" were set up, as well as public welfare associations, sanitation committees, associations for the collection of clothing and blankets for the needy, etc. The Jewish will to live confronted the Nazi extermination plan. Rabbi Itzhak Nissenbaum of the Warsaw ghetto expressed it cogently by speaking of *kiddush ha-hayim* (sanctification of life): "Now is the time for the sanctification of life [*kiddush ha-hayim*] and not for the Sanctification of God's Name [*kiddush ha-shem*] through death. Once when our enemies demanded our soul, the Jew martyred his body for *kiddush ha-shem*. Today when the enemy demands the body, it is the Jew's obligation to defend himself, to preserve his life."

104

105

106

107

108. Jews from Lodz, Poland, on their way to the ghetto.

109. Radom ghetto. The sign warns: "Danger of Epidemics. Jewish Residential District" and details punishments for entering or leaving the ghetto without legitimate authorisation.

110. Warsaw Jews being forced to build the walls of the ghetto.

MAP OF LODZ GHETTO

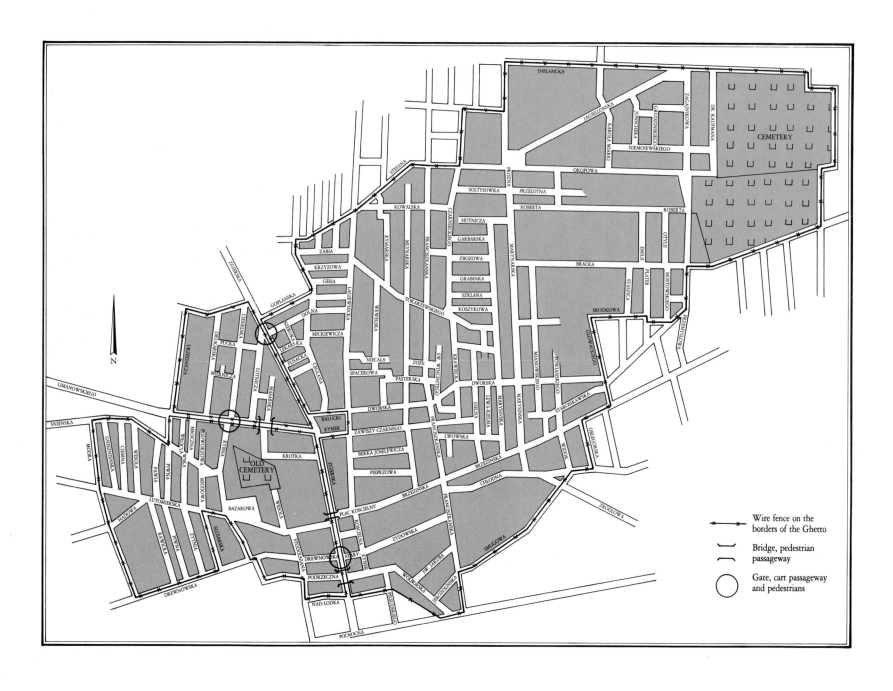

Wire fence on the borders of the Ghetto

Bridge, pedestrian passageway

Gate, cart passageway and pedestrians

111. Jews on their way to the Lodz ghetto, Poland.

112

112. Jews on their way to the Lodz
ghetto, Poland.

113. Jews immediately after being
interned in the Lodz ghetto, Poland.

114. Lodz ghetto, Poland: wooden bridge connecting the two sections of the ghetto.

115

115. Lublin ghetto, Poland: water carrier.

116. Lublin ghetto, Poland: street scene.

117. Lublin ghetto, Poland: queuing up for the water ration.

MAP OF WARSAW GHETTO
1940–1941

Jewish Residential District, out of bound to German troops according to the German edict of 7.8.40.

The borders of the Ghetto as of November 15, 1940 (the day of the creation of the Ghetto).

Changes in the borders of the Ghetto made February–April 1941.

0   500 m   1000 m

118. Typical scene from the Warsaw ghetto.

MAP OF WARSAW GHETTO
1942-1943

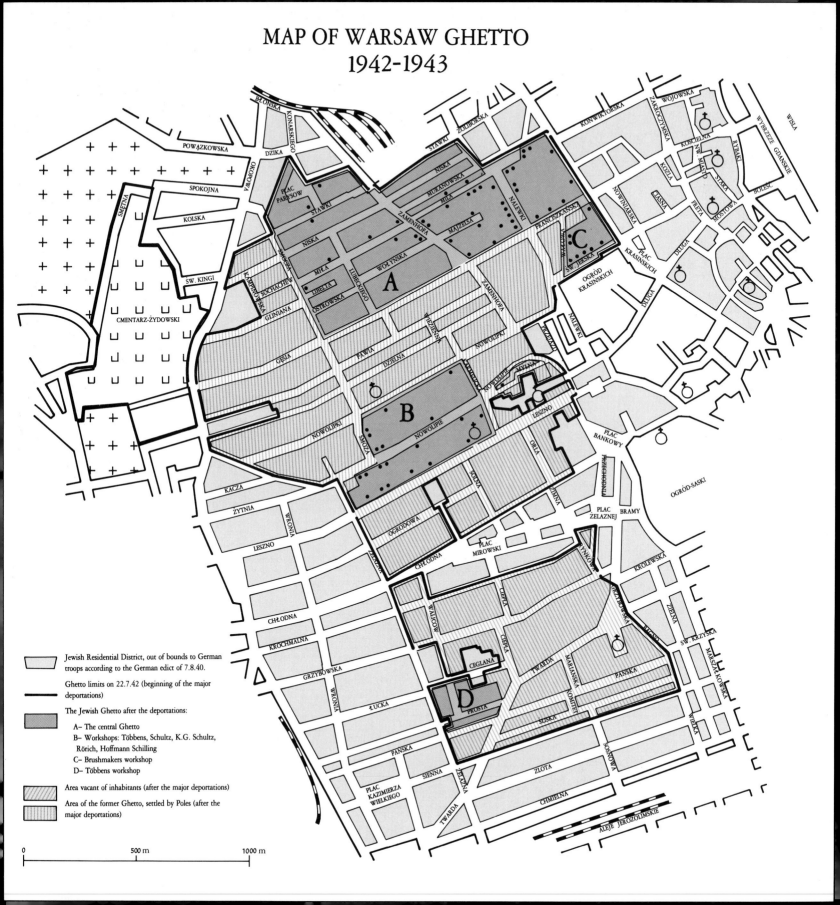

Jewish Residential District, out of bounds to German troops according to the German edict of 7.8.40.

Ghetto limits on 22.7.42 (beginning of the major deportations)

The Jewish Ghetto after the deportations:

A– The central Ghetto
B– Workshops: Többens, Schultz, K.G. Schultz, Rörich, Hoffmann Schilling
C– Brushmakers workshop
D– Többens workshop

Area vacant of inhabitants (after the major deportations)

Area of the former Ghetto, settled by Poles (after the major deportations)

0   500 m   1000 m

119. Warsaw ghetto: Jewish child begging for alms.

120. Warsaw ghetto: a busy
street. The signs on the shops
predate the ghetto. In the center,
a tram with the Star of David.

121

121. Warsaw ghetto: a street cobbler at work.

122. Warsaw ghetto: woman peddler.

123. Warsaw ghetto: a busy street market (overleaf).

116

124

124, 125. Warsaw ghetto: children in rags.

126

126, 127. Warsaw ghetto: child and
adult street musicians trying to earn a living.

Education and Culture

Isolated from the surrounding population, subject to wanton violence, exposed to hunger and disease, the Jews struggled to preserve some vestiges of their humanity. In some places, the Germans allowed the establishment of educational institutions; in others, underground schools were formed. The larger ghettos boasted schools with Hebrew and Yiddish as the language of instruction, as well as religious schools and *Talmud Torah*s. Highschool-age children subject to forced labor duty studied in evening classes and took vocational courses. The terrible congestion made it virtually impossible to find suitable classrooms. Frequently rooms that served as sleeping quarters at night served as classrooms during the day.

In addition to education, the ghettos engendered and promoted various forms of cultural activities. In some ghettos, theater companies, choirs and orchestras were established. Performances by schoolchildren were organized to celebrate Jewish festivals such as *Hanukkah, Purim, Tu B'Shvat* and others. Libraries circulated books which had been assembled with great effort. Reading was a very popular pastime in the ghetto. The best specialists and scholars in various fields were recruited to give public lectures on assorted subjects and to teach courses for adults.

Religious life

Devout Jews in the ghetto continued to observe the Sabbath and Jewish holy days, study Torah, and provide religious education for their children. Jewish religious observance under ghetto conditions posed a formidable task. In many places the Germans outlawed public worship. Synagogues located within the ghetto were turned into dormitories for homeless refugees, making it well-nigh impossible to hold religious services in them. Shortages and hunger in the ghetto made observance of *kashrut* nearly impossible. However, some exceptionally devout Jews preferred to starve rather than eat the forbidden food. For their part, the Nazis did not honor the Sabbath or other Jewish festivals and ghetto residents were required to do forced labor on those days. Some of the most cruel actions against Jews were carried out by the Germans especially on Jewish holidays.

Political parties and youth movements

Nearly all Jewish political parties and youth movements active before the war continued their activities clandestinely in the ghettos. Zionist youth movements operated their own educational networks and trained their members for life in the Land of Israel. The German occupation failed to extinguish all hopes of making *aliyah*. In general, each party and youth movement looked after its members by rendering welfare assistance, finding jobs and combating hunger. They also set up an extensive underground press network which supplied information about developments on the war fronts, world news, reports about events outside the ghetto walls in Poland, etc. The main source of information was radio broadcasts received on radio sets operated clandestinely within the ghetto at great risk. The underground press also supplied information about developments in the ghetto, printed comments on current events, and often sharply criticized actions of the Judenräte. It also served as an educational–political instrument for the expression of the views of its publishers. Its main task, however, was to boost the morale of ghetto residents by encouraging them to carry on their struggle for survival. In the course of time the political parties and youth movements became a significant factor in ghetto life, forcing the Judenräte to take their views and reactions into consideration.

128

129. Warsaw ghetto: clandestine Torah study.

130. Young worshipper in a ghetto synagogue. Such synagogues also served as living quarters for refugees.

131

132

131. Lodz ghetto, Poland: children being taught the geography of Palestine.

132. Warsaw ghetto: children's choir.

133. Warsaw ghetto: entrance to a theater.

133

134. Warsaw ghetto: workshop.

135. Warsaw ghetto: vocational training center to increase productivity in the ghetto.

134

135

138

136. Warsaw ghetto: mattresses produced in the ghetto being delivered to the Germans.

137. Lodz ghetto, Poland: Jews pulling a cart with products made in the ghetto.

138. Dombrowa ghetto, Poland: sewing workshop.

139. Elderly couple in the Warsaw ghetto.

140, 141. Warsaw ghetto:
medical treatment.

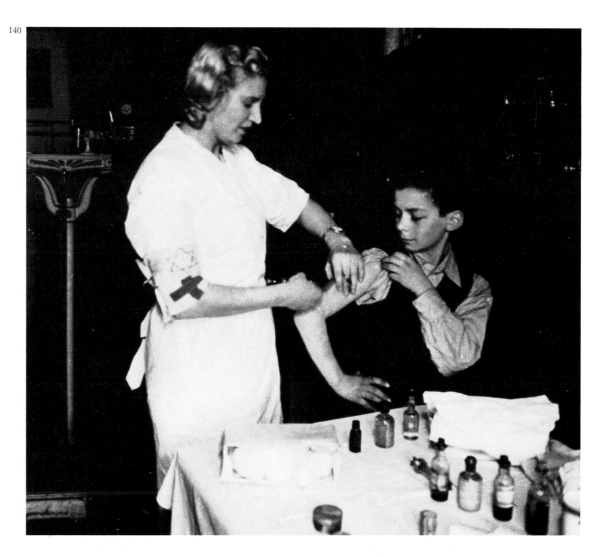

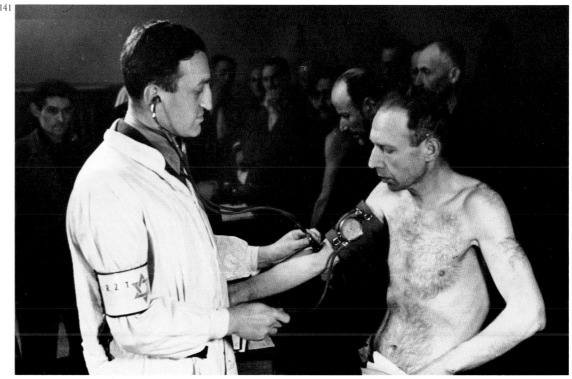

142. Lodz ghetto, Poland: soup kitchen.

143. Warsaw ghetto: lunch in a Jewish orphanage.

144. Lodz ghetto, Poland: children entering a soup kitchen.

145. Warsaw ghetto: Jewish child dying on the sidewalk.

146. Warsaw ghetto: woman selling hot soup.

147. Warsaw ghetto: victims of starvation.

148

148. Warsaw ghetto: Jewish children caught by the Nazis smuggling food into the ghetto.

149. Lodz ghetto, Poland: Jews digging for leavings of potatoes and other vegetables.

150. Lodz ghetto, Poland: outside a soup kitchen.

149

150

151

151. Lodz ghetto, Poland: bread being
delivered for distribution of the daily
ration.

152. Warsaw ghetto: transportation of
the sick.

152

153. Warsaw ghetto: woman beggar.

154. Warsaw ghetto: child begging for food.

155

156

157

150

158

159

152

160

161

162

154

163

164

165

167. A meager meal in the Kutno ghetto, Poland.

168

169

The last journey: death and burial in the Warsaw ghetto
169–176

170

171

172

173

174

175

176

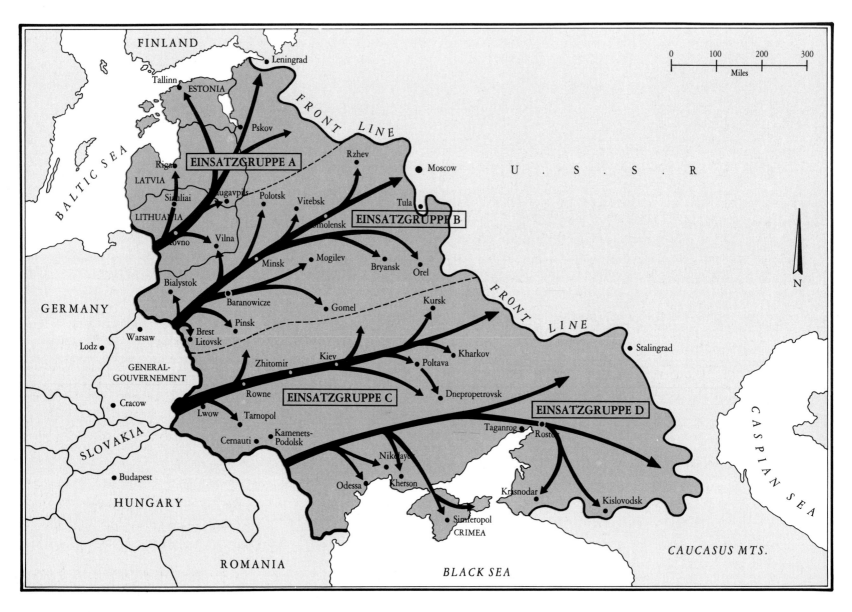

German–Soviet frontier as of September 1939

Paths of the Einsatzgruppen, July 1941–1943

Area occupied in German advance

U.S.S.R. Area

MASS MURDER
1941–1945

Einsatzgruppen operations in the occupied territories of the Soviet Union

The invasion of the Soviet Union by Nazi Germany on June 22, 1941 opened a new and final stage in Nazi policy toward the Jews, the so-called "Final Solution of the Jewish Question." It was to last until the surrender of Germany on May 8, 1945. During this stage millions of Jews were murdered in mass executions carried out at shooting pits and in the gas chambers of extermination camps.

The decision to undertake the mass extermination of the Jews was adopted prior to the invasion of the Soviet Union. As far as we know, it was taken in stages. At first the Jews of the Soviet Union were consigned to wholesale slaughter. Later the scope of extermination was expanded to embrace all European Jews. The decision to embark on a course of mass extermination must be viewed as part of the process of a further radicalization of Nazi policy toward the Jews. As the war expanded, nearly all previously existing international and political constraints fell away. However, apart from this general trend in Nazi anti-Jewish policy, the extermination decision adopted on the eve of the attack on the Soviet Union stemmed also from Hitler's view of the role played by the Jews in the Soviet Union. He regarded the Jews as the moving force in the Soviet power structure, working to exploit the Soviet state to achieve their goals of world domination. As the excerpt from his speech to the Reichstag on January 30, 1939 demonstrates (see above), he did not bother to conceal this view. Consequently, for him the physical liquidation of the Jews was tantamount to the elimination of the ideological and material threat posed by the Soviet state.

The existing documents reveal in broad outline the process of decision-making on the "final solution" to be carried out on Soviet territory and the operative directives issued in this regard. On March 13, 1941, in the course of preparations for the planned invasion of the Soviet Union (code-named "Barbarossa)," the High Command of the German army issued several directives including the following:

> Within the area of army operations, the *Reichsführer–SS* [Himmler] will be entrusted, on behalf of the Führer [Hitler], with *special tasks* for the preparation of the political administration — tasks which derive from the *decisive struggle* that will have to be carried out between the two opposing political systems.

The term "decisive struggle" implied that terms of international treaties and conventions concerning the conduct of warfare, treatment of POWs and of the civilian population, etc., would not apply in the projected invasion of the Soviet Union. "Special tasks" referred to mass extermination of political commissars and Jews. A more explicit reference to the inapplicability of international codes of warfare in the conflict with the Soviet Union is to be found in the "Commissars' Order" issued by the German army on June 6, 1941 and in written and oral directives issued by Heydrich to senior SS officers shortly before the invasion.

In preparation of the invasion of the Soviet Union and in order to carry out the "special tasks," i.e. the murder of Jews and Communist activists, assigned by Hitler to Himmler and the SS, four *Einsatzgruppen* (special units) of the SS were set up in Germany. Subordinated directly to Heydrich, the *Einsatzgruppen* were each the size of a battalion (500 to 900 men). The total strength of the *Einsatzgruppen* was about 3,000 men. Their operational units were *Einsatzkommandos* of company size. The invading German forces advanced rapidly eastward. By the winter of 1941, they reached the outskirts of Leningrad in Northern Russia, approached Moscow in the central sector, and drove toward the cities of Kharkov and Rostov-on-Don in the south. However in the winter of 1941–42, the German army suffered serious setbacks, and its offensive was repulsed on several fronts, particularly the Moscow and Rostov areas. In spring 1942 it resumed its advance on the southern front, reaching Stalingrad and Northern Caucasus.

With the invasion of the Soviet Union the *Einsatzgruppen* of the SS moved directly behind the advance units of the German forces. *Einsatzgruppe* A operated in the Baltic republics and along the line of advance toward Leningrad; *Einsatzgruppe* B was assigned to Byelorussia and the Moscow axis; *Einsatzgruppe* C fanned out over the Ukraine toward Kiev and Kharkov; *Einsatzgruppe* D was active in the Southern Ukraine, along the Black Sea shores toward Crimea and the Caucasus. In addition to the *Einsatzgruppen,* the mopping up operations and killing of Jews also involved several *Waffen*–SS formations which operated in the Polesie marshes and in Southern Byelorussia.

Most Soviet Jews were concentrated in the areas overrun by the Germans. These were the areas included in the Pale of Settlement, territory where Jews had been given permission to settle by the Czarist governments in pre-revolutionary Russia. The territories annexed by the Soviet Union in 1939–1940 were inhabited by close to 1.9

million Jews: about 1.3 million in Western Byelorussia and Western Ukraine; 250,000 in Lithuania, Latvia and Estonia; and 325,000 in Bessarabia and North Bukovina. To this number one must add about 250,000 Jewish refugees who fled there from Nazi-occupied Poland in 1939. Due to the rapid advance of the German forces, about 12% of the Jewish population managed to flee eastward. Another 1–2% had been exiled by the Soviet authorities to the Soviet interior for "political" or "class" reasons prior to the Nazi invasion. Altogether about 300,000 Jewish inhabitants or refugees succeeded in escaping Nazi clutches. Over 1.8 million Jews who lived in the areas annexed by the USSR fell into their hands.

In addition to the Jews who lived in the annexed territories, some 2.2 million Jews lived within the 1939 borders of the Soviet Union in areas occupied by Germany. With the Nazi troops rapidly advancing, the Soviets undertook an evacuation of the general population, the staffs of various state institutions, and factories. We may estimate that over half the Jewish population living within the pre-September 1939 Soviet borders slipped away. The remaining 1 to 1.1 million Soviet Jews were overwhelmed by the Nazi machinery of destruction. In all, 2.8–2.9 million Jews who lived within the June 1941 Soviet borders found themselves under Nazi rule.

Wherever they operated, the *Einsatzgruppen* found thousands of willing local collaborators who took part in the killing of Jews. Local cooperation was particularly extensive in the Baltic countries of Lithuania, Latvia and Estonia and in the Western Ukraine, where it took the form of assistance in rounding up Jews and even participation in mass killings. The German military administration in the occupied areas also rendered assistance. Immediately after occupying a locality, the German army issued

177

orders requiring the registration of all local Jews and their wearing of a yellow badge to set them apart from the native population and to mark them for easy identification by the *Einsatzgruppen*. It also issued orders for the formation of the Judenräte. In some places the military administration ordered the concentration of Jews in temporary ghettos until their liquidation by the *Einsatzgruppen*.

The standard method employed by the *Einsatzgruppen* in killing operations included removing the Jews from their homes and marching them to pits not far from the town which had been dug in advance, or to anti-tank ditches dug previously by the Soviets as part of the defence lines. Occasionally, the victims had to dig the pits themselves. Thereupon they were lined up in groups at the edge of the pits and shot. When the killing was over, the pits would be covered with dirt.

At the Nuremberg trials, Otto Dohlendorf, chief of *Einsatzgruppe* D, explained the way his unit acquitted itself of its tasks:

> The unit would enter a village or city and order the prominent Jewish citizens to call together all the Jews for the purpose of resettlement. They were ordered to hand over their valuables to the leader of the unit, and shortly before execution to surrender their outer clothing. The men, women and children were led to a place of execution which in most cases was located next to a deeply-excavated anti-tank ditch. Then they were shot, kneeling or standing, and the corpses thrown into the ditch. . . . The unit commanders, or persons especially assigned for that purpose, had to fire their last bullets at those victims who were still alive.

In their rapid advance eastward, the *Einsatzgruppen* left behind a trail of killing sites with hundreds of thousands of Jewish victims: the mass grave at Romboli near Riga; the Ninth Fort at Kovno; the village of Ponar near Vilna; Maly-Trostenets near Minsk; Babi-Yar in Kiev; and hundreds of other localities throughout the occupied Soviet territory. In 1942 the Germans set up a special unit, Commando 1005, whose task was to open the mass graves and incinerate the bodies of the murdered victims so as to obliterate all traces of the crimes. This unit was active until the withdrawal of the Germans from the Soviet Union in 1944.

As the invasion forces continued to advance eastward, the rear areas of the occupied Soviet Union were placed under a civilian administration headed by Alfred Rosenberg, who had been appointed Minister for the Occupied Territories in the East. The transfer was effected step-by-step between August and October, 1941. The areas in question included Lithuania, Latvia, Estonia, Western Byelorussia and the city of Minsk, all of which were named "Reichskommissariat Ostland," and all of the Ukraine west of the river Dnieper, called "Reichskommissariat Ukraine." The region of Transnistria, comprising parts of the Ukraine between the rivers Bug and Dniester, were transferred to Romanian rule. Some 150,000 Jews from Bessarabia and Northern Bukovina were expelled to Transnistria; thousands of them died on the way and later of hunger and disease in the ghettos. Part of the Western Ukraine, including the city of

178. German soldiers. Russia, June, 1941.

179. German soldiers attacking a Russian village, June, 1941.

Lvov, was incorporated into the General Government of Poland. The local Jews shared the fate of other General Government Jews: most were murdered in extermination camps (mainly at Belzec), while others were shot near their places of residence. The Bialystok–Grodno area became a separate and independent administrative region connected to the German administration in East Prussia.

The *Einsatzgruppen* failed to complete their killing operations in the western areas of the Soviet Union before their transfer to the civil administration. Most of the Jewish inhabitants were incarcerated in ghettos and the task of continuing the killings was assigned to units of the Security Police and the SD subordinate to the civil administration. In this phase the liquidation proceeded with the extensive cooperation of local auxiliary police units and detachments of local volunteers. The method of killing was the same as used by the *Einsatzgruppen*: execution in shooting pits. Killing operations continued through the fall and winter of 1941; in parts of Byelorussia and the Ukraine under civil administration, they were carried out mostly in the spring and summer of 1942.

By the end of 1941, with the killing of Jews proceeding apace, the Germans realized that the war against the Soviet Union was not going to be won so quickly. Consequently, they undertook to organize the rear areas in anticipation of protracted warfare at the front. This led to the need for a large labor force, particularly skilled workers, many of whom were Jews. The German civil administration, supported by the army but often over the objections of the SS, decided to permit the continued existence of ghettos in larger cities such as Vilna, Kovno, Riga, Minsk, Lida and other places where Jewish skilled workers were employed in enterprises vital for the war effort. These ghettos continued to exist until the summer of 1943, when Himmler ordered their liquidation. Part of the ghetto residents, mostly women, children and the aged, were shot near their places of residence, whereas others from the ghettos of Minsk, Lida and Vilna were sent to the extermination camp at Sobibor. Able-bodied men and women were sent to concentration camps in Latvia and Estonia. Shortly before the German withdrawal from these areas in the summer of 1944, these camps were liquidated together with their inmates. Only a handful of Soviet Jews who were under the Nazi rule eluded the clutches of the Nazi machinery of destruction and survived until the end of the war.

180. Jewish girl abused by Ukrainian mobs.

181. Lvov, Ukraine, shortly after its occupation by German troops, July, 1941. Ukrainians dragging Jews through the streets.

182. Murder of Jews in Kovno, Lithuania, end of June, 1941. The perpetrators are Lithuanians, the onlookers — Germans.

182

183

184

185. Kovno, Fort VII: mass execution of Jews.

186

186. Ponar, Lithuania: mass execution of Jews from Vilna. General view of the pit in which Jews were kept before being taken to the execution site.

187. Ponar, Lithuania: mass execution of Jews from Vilna (detail from photo no. 186).

188. Ponar, Lithuania: mass execution of Jews from Vilna (detail from photo no. 186). Blindfolded Jews cling to one another while being led to their execution by the killing squad.

187

188

189

189, 190, 191.
Jassy, Romania: pogrom staged by Romanian mobs, June 29–July 3/4, 1941, during which some ten thousand Jews were brutally murdered.

192, 193. Executions carried out by Einsatzgruppen in the occupied areas of the Soviet Union during 1941/1942 (exact location unknown).

190

191

182

192

193

194. Mass execution of Jews from the Sdolbunov area, Ukraine, 14 October, 1942.

195. Naked Jewish men before their execution.

194

196

197

196. Vinica, Ukraine: the last Jew alive
being shot.

197. Jews digging their own graves
before being shot by the Germans.

198. Execution carried out by
Einsatzgruppen in the occupied areas of
the Soviet Union during 1941/1942.

199. Jewish mother before execution, Byelorussia (exact location unknown).

200. Liepaja, Latvia: Jewish women before their execution.

201

201, 202, 203. Liepaja, Latvia: Jewish
women before their execution.

192

204

204, 205. A group of Jewish women, some with babies in their arms, before their execution in Misocz, Ukraine. The photos show local collaborators assisting the Germans in their murderous work.

194

205

206

207

208

196

209

206, 207, 208. A series of photos from the
Ciezanow ghetto. Jews were forced to watch the
hanging of five of their coreligionists in the
courtyard of the castle.

209. Bodies of murdered Jews (location unknown).

210

211

212

213. German soldier shooting at woman with child in her arms (location unknown).

DEPORTATIONS
TO DEATH CAMPS

MAP OF THE DEATH CAMPS
In the Nazi Occupied Territories

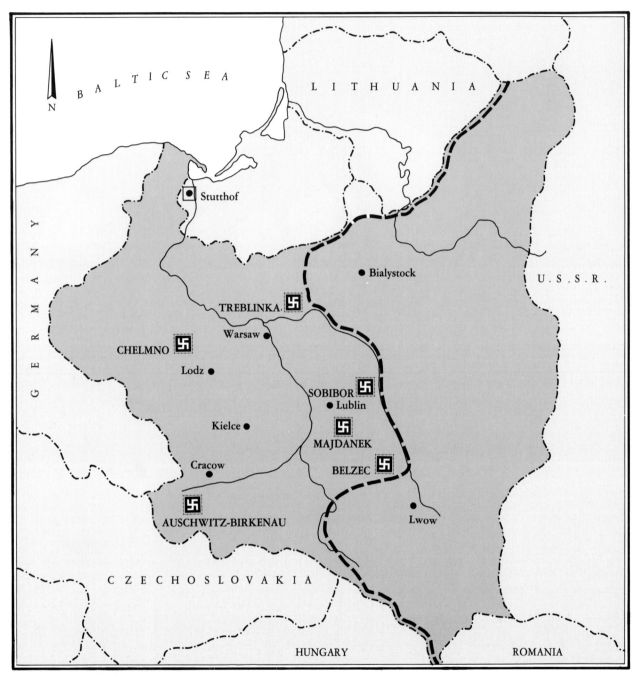

Partition of Poland between Nazi-Germany and the Soviet Union

Death Camp

Concentration Camp

Ghetto

Poland before 1939 partition

DEPORTATIONS TO DEATH CAMPS

Preparations for the extermination of Jews throughout Europe

Within a few weeks of the German invasion of the Soviet Union, with the killing operations of the *Einsatzgruppen* moving into high gear, the Nazis began preparations for the extermination of other European Jews. On July 31, 1941, Goering issued an order addressed to Heydrich. It stated, *inter alia*:

> I herewith charge you with making all necessary preparations with regard to organizational, practical and financial aspects for an *overall solution* (*Gesamtlösung*) of the Jewish question in the German sphere of influence in Europe. . . . I further charge you with submitting to me promptly an overall plan of the preliminary organizational, practical and financial measures for the execution of the intended *Final Solution* (*Endlösung*) of the Jewish question.

To coordinate the preparations for the implementation of this task, Heydrich called a conference in Wannsee (a suburb of Berlin) to be held on January 20, 1942, and attended by representatives of various Reich ministries, chiefs of German administration in the occupied European countries, and senior SS officers including Adolf Eichmann, chief of the Gestapo's Jewish section. The Wannsee Conference took place following significant political and military developments throughout the world.

On December 11, 1941, in the aftermath of the Japanese attack on Pearl Harbor, Germany declared war against the United States. The war had assumed worldwide and total proportions, dividing all of humanity between the Allied powers and the Axis powers. The new situation released the Germans from all constraints associated with political considerations and the adverse reaction of world public opinion that the mass murder of Jews might have been likely to arouse.

The Wannsee Conference proceedings were recorded and its entire protocol submitted as evidence to the International War Crimes Tribunal in Nuremberg. Heydrich opened the conference with the announcement of his appointment by Goering as Plenipotentiary for the Preparations of the Final Solution of the Jewish Question in Europe. Further on, he said:

Emigration has now been replaced by evacuation of the Jews to the East as a further possible solution, with the appropriate prior authorization by the Führer. . . . In the course of this Final Solution of the European Jewish question, approximately 11 million Jews must be taken into consideration, distributed over the individual countries as follows . . ."

At this point Heydrich presented a list of 33 countries and regions in Europe with the number of Jews in each of them. Apart from countries already under occupation by Germany or its allies, the list included countries the Germans planned to occupy such as England, all of the European part of the Soviet Union, as well as neutral countries, such as Portugal, Spain, Sweden, Switzerland, Ireland and Turkey.

Practical preparations for the genocide of the Jewish people were undertaken simultaneously with organizational preparations led by Heydrich. In the summer of 1941, Himmler summoned Rudolf Hoess, commander of the Auschwitz concentration camp. In his testimony after the war Hoess revealed that at their meeting Himmler informed him of Hitler's decision to undertake the final solution of the Jewish question. He went on to say that in view of the fact that the methods employed in the East (the murder of Jews in the occupied Soviet Union) were no longer suitable for the assigned task, the camp of Auschwitz must be made ready for the job of extermination. Shortly after this meeting Eichmann arrived in Auschwitz. He and Hoess came to the conclusion that mass extermination could be effected only by means of gas, since the method of shooting Jews as practiced in the Soviet Union was not suitable for liquidating large numbers of people within a short time.

Killing by gas was not a new idea in Nazi Germany. It had been used in the Euthanasia (mercy killing) Program; between 70,000 and 90,000 mental patients and seriously disabled persons, nearly all of them Germans and a few Jews, had been gassed between September 1939 and late August 1941. Nazis viewed the Euthanasia Program as a way of improving Aryan racial stock and of ridding the country of "parasites and expendables," as they defined them. Hitler set up a secret organization for this purpose, the so-called T-4, responsible directly to his chancellery. This organization operated various "medical" institutions staffed by physicians entrusted with determining which patients suffered from incurable diseases and must be liquidated. The victims were ushered into an hermetically-sealed room located in each of these "medical" institutions, and asphyxiated by gas. Their bodies were then burned in special crematoria. Information about euthanasia gassings soon leaked out, giving rise to pressure, particularly from the victims' relatives and the Church, to stop these killings. Hitler yielded and at the end of August 1941, he ordered a temporary halt to these

Land	Zahl
A. Altreich	131.800
Ostmark	43.700
Ostgebiete	420.000
Generalgouvernement	2.284.000
Bialystok	400.000
Protektorat Böhmen und Mähren	74.200
Estland — judenfrei —	
Lettland	3.500
Litauen	34.000
Belgien	43.000
Dänemark	5.600
Frankreich / Besetztes Gebiet	165.000
Unbesetztes Gebiet	700.000
Griechenland	69.600
Niederlande	160.800
Norwegen	1.300
B. Bulgarien	48.000
England	330.000
Finnland	2.300
Irland	4.000
Italien einschl. Sardinien	58.000
Albanien	200
Kroatien	40.000
Portugal	3.000
Rumänien einschl. Bessarabien	342.000
Schweden	8.000
Schweiz	18.000
Serbien	10.000
Slowakei	88.000
Spanien	6.000
Türkei (europ. Teil)	55.500
Ungarn	742.800
UdSSR	5.000.000
Ukraine 2.994.684	
Weißrußland ausschl. Bialystok 446.484	
Zusammen: über	**11.000.000**

A page from the Wannsee Conference Protocol.

medical killings. However, the experience gathered in the course of the Euthanasia Program served the SS authorities charged with preparations for the "Final Solution."

The first experiments with gassing as a method of extermination were conducted at Auschwitz in September 1941. The subjects were a group of Soviet POWs. They were locked in a sealed cellar and gassed by Zyklon-B. The prisoners choked to death within a very short time. A series of further experiments followed which enabled the Nazis to develop this new method of killing. At the same time the *Einsatzgruppen* developed a similar method with the help of the Technical Section attached to Heydrich's headquarters. Here gas vans were used instead of gas chambers. A van would be fitted with an hermetically-sealed rear compartment; from the outside it resembled an ambulance or refrigerator van. A special pipe was fitted from the exhaust pipe to the compartment so that the carbon monoxide of the exhaust fumes went directly into the sealed compartment. The victims would be loaded into the compartment, the door locked, and the engine started. Within a half hour's drive all the victims were gassed to death. When the van arrived at a designated site, the doors were opened and the corpses removed and buried. Large vans could contain 150 victims, smaller ones about half that number. In the last months of 1941, these gas vans were used to exterminate thousands of Jews in the occupied Soviet areas.

The first extermination camp began functioning on December 8, 1941, near the village of Chelmno in the Lodz district in occupied Poland. The Jews were killed by means of gas vans. The victims were usually brought by trains and unloaded in the vicinity of the camp, at the center of which stood an old and crumbling palace partly surrounded by a park. After being led into a fenced-off area, the victims were informed that they would be driven in vans to the showers before being sent to work. They were told to undress and climb into the vans. After a drive of approximately four kilometers, all the people inside had been poisoned by the exhaust fumes. The vans completed their journey at a fenced site in the woods. A group of Jewish prisoners kept there especially for that task would remove the bodies and bury them. Later the bodies were disposed of by incineration. Three such gas vans operated in Chelmno. Staffed by some 150 police and SS men, the Chelmno camp operated until April 1943, when it was temporarily closed. In the spring of 1944, it resumed operations for three more months. Altogether close to 300,000 Jews brought there from Lodz and other areas and a few groups of Gypsies were murdered in the camp.

In November 1941, preparations were launched for the extermination of the Jews in the General Government. The figures supplied by Heydrich at the Wannsee Conference put their number at 2,284,000. Later this venture was code-named by the Germans "Operation Reinhard" (after Heydrich who was assassinated by the Czech underground in May 1942). Odilo Globocnik, then SS and Police Leader of the Lublin district, was appointed commander of the operation which was to be carried out in three extermination camps. The first, at Belzec, was established in mid-March 1942; the second, at Sobibor, became operational in May 1942; and the third, in Treblinka, began functioning in the last week of July 1942. These three camps, all situated alongside the eastern frontier of the General Government, were fitted with permanent gas chambers. The gas, carbon monoxide, was piped in from gasoline or diesel engines installed outside the chambers. Each camp was staffed by 25 to 30 Germans, mostly recruited from among the Euthanasia Program employees, and 90 to 120 Ukrainians, most of whom were Soviet POWs who had volunteered to serve the Germans. The latter were assembled and trained for their jobs at the SS training camp in Trawniki near Lublin; local inhabitants called them "Trawniki men."

The largest concentration and extermination camp, Auschwitz, was established in the Silesia region in Poland, which had been incorporated into the Reich. As early as 1940, a concentration camp was set up on the premises of a former army camp in the vicinity of the village of Auschwitz (*Oswiecim* in Polish). At first it served as a camp for captured Polish officers and political prisoners. Numerous labor camps employing prisoners, including a subsidiary of the German armaments firm I.G. Farben, were set up in the vicinity of the Auschwitz camp, to which they were subordinate. In October 1941, work began on the construction of a camp in the village of Birkenau (*Brzezinka* in Polish), called Auschwitz II, the largest of all the extermination camps. It lay some two miles west of the main camp, Auschwitz I. Birkenau started functioning in March 1942. The four gas chambers of Auschwitz II operating on Zyklon-B gas had the capacity to kill 12,000 people at one time. Bodies of the murdered victims were then burned in crematoria located in the same structure that contained the gas chambers. Eight thousand bodies could be burned there in 24 hours; whenever the number of gassed victims exceeded this figure on a given day, the remaining bodies were burned on pyres in the woods near the gas chambers. The last gassing action in Auschwitz took place at the end of October 1944. The two camps were staffed by some 2,500 SS men. Auschwitz I and II functioned until January 1945, by which time 1.8 to 2.0 million people had been murdered there, including 1.3 to 1.5 million Jews.

The extermination camps of Chelmno, Belzec, Sobibor and Treblinka served as death factories. The victims were brought straight to the gas chambers. Several hundred Jewish prisoners removed from the death transports were kept on hand to process the corpses and the victims' belongings. Each such contingent was summarily murdered every few weeks or months. The camp of Majdanek, near Lublin, was essentially a concentration camp for both Jews and non-Jews. Other camps in the Lublin district functioned as Majdanek's subsidiaries. Scores of thousands of Jews were murdered there, or passed through, or were kept as prisoners, including Jewish POWs who had served in the Polish army. Only a handful of them survived.

The extermination camp of Auschwitz–Birkenau served also as a concentration camp. Some of the death transports arriving there were subjected to "selections" in the course of which young and strong men were picked out of the transport and put to work in the camp or sent to other camps. Other candidates for selection were children, twins, hunchbacks, and others who were picked out for medical experiments conducted there by German physicians, the most notorious of whom was Dr. Josef Mengele. Prisoners left alive were not exempt from "selections"; several times a day roll-calls took place for the purpose of ferreting out the weak, sick or unfit for work who were then sent to the gas chambers. Prisoners lived on borrowed time under a most strict regime. Hunger, a punishment system which included flogging, exercises aimed at exhausting prisoners to death, and all sorts of brutalities limited only by the imagination of the SS men, were their daily fare. Dozens of dead bodies were removed daily from the prisoners' barracks. Only a handful managed to hold out in Auschwitz–Birkenau.

The deportations

The deportation of Jews from throughout Europe to the extermination camps in occupied Poland was a colossal operation. Its execution required detailed planning, organizational facilities on a huge scale, and an immense logistical apparatus. A wide range of German institutions and organizations was involved in the deportations. The operation was headed by Heydrich and, after his assassination in May 1942, by Ernst Kaltenbrunner, Heydrich's successor as chief of the Reich Security Main Office. It involved various SS agencies, civil authorities in charge of various occupied areas, the German army, and governing bodies in Nazi satellite states. The German Rail Authority took part in the deportations by supplying the means of transport for conveying Jewish victims to the camps. It should be noted that despite the great need of the military for trains, the allocation of rail transport for carrying Jews to the death camps ranked higher on the Nazi list of priorities. Plans for deportation from all European countries also specified at which of the five extermination camps a given transport would arrive. This necessitated a precise timetable so as to preclude the arrival of several transports to the same destination at the same time. The planners also had to take into account the capacity of each extermination facility so that no transport would arrive at a camp whose gas chambers were incapable of gassing all the victims within a short time.

Deportations of Jews were carried out in secret and involved a great deal of camouflage and deception. The deportees were told they would be sent to work somewhere in the East. For Polish Jews this meant being deported to Nazi-occupied Soviet territories. Jews from other countries believed they were being sent to work in occupied Poland. The Germans endeavored to sustain these beliefs and hopes by forcing some of the deportees to send postcards *en route* to the camps, or even after their arrival there, to the families they had left behind in their countries of origin. The postcards informed the victims' families that the deportees were alive and well, and that they had arrived at a labor camp. Several hours later the senders were no longer among the living.

The method and phases of the deportation operation were similar in most places. Usually the deportation order came without warning. The would-be deportees were

214. The gate to Auschwitz–Birkenau.

208

given very short notice — several hours to a few days. Sometimes rumors of the impending deportation reached the victims several weeks earlier. First the Jews were served with a notice to leave their homes and assemble at an appointed spot, usually situated in the vicinity of the railway station. They had to leave beind nearly all their possessions and were allowed to take only hand luggage. Occasionally, the Germans determined the maximum weight of a parcel; usually it could not exceed 10 to 15 kilograms per person. Those who believed they were going to work took tools with them, in addition to clothing, kitchen utensils and bedding. Laden with parcels and bundles, the Jews often marched many kilometers, children and elderly among them, to the railway station. Those who stayed behind were shot on the spot, the sick and discovered hideaways among them. In some places the elderly and the sick were conveyed on horse-driven carts hired from neighboring villages, or even on trucks. When the deportation ranged over an area with several small ghettos, they would sometimes be combined, with the deportees forming a column several kilometers long. Marches to the railway stations took place in any weather: cold and rain in fall and winter, or scorching sun in summer.

Jewish reaction to deportations was affected by a number of factors. Those who had been incarcerated for several years in the ghetto, in conditions of hunger, disease, terror and victimization, tended to accept the deportation order with resignation mingled with despair. Unrestrained terror unleashed by the Germans in the course of the deportations shocked and numbed their victims, crushing their will to resist or escape. Furthermore, the overwhelming majority of the deported Jews did, in fact, believe they were being sent to work "somewhere in the East." They even hoped that with their resettlement in the East they would be able to work so that their conditions would be better than in the ghettos they were leaving behind. This was only to be expected. After all, who would have envisioned that innocent people, including children and the aged, men and women, would be taken away to be murdered only because they were Jews? Nothing resembling such a thorough extermination had ever taken place before.

In addition to the Germans, local police detachments also took part in the deportations: Polish "blue police," Dutch "green police," French, Romanian and Hungarian gendarmerie, Ukrainian, Lithuanian, Latvian and Estonian police units, and other local formations in every country from where Jews were being deported. Deportations were witnessed by the local non-Jewish inhabitants who looked on from doorsteps or sidewalks. Some faces bore the expression of sorrow and sympathy, others expressed glee, but the majority watched the tragic spectacle of the expulsion of neighbors and acquaintances with indifference, as if unaffected by it all.

Upon arrival at the railway station the Jews were packed into sealed freight cars. Frequently, 100 to 150 people, sometimes even more, were compressed into one freight car suitable for carrying half that number. With all the deportees inside, the cars were locked from the outside and an escort of German and/or local policemen guarded

215

215. Drohobycz, Western Ukraine:
deportation of Jews to the Belzec death
camp, March–November 1942.

the train until its arrival at the camp gates. The journey, which under normal conditions should have lasted several hours, often took days. Military trains moving eastward to the Soviet front were given priority over the deportation transports, which often were shunted on sidings for hours on end, waiting for permission to resume their journey. Congestion beyond description, lack of any santitation facilities, with people relieving themselves inside the cars into buckets or on the floor, lack of air and water, blistering heat in the summer or sub-zero temperatures in the winter, caused scores of deaths en route. Sometimes transports, particularly from ghettos in Poland, arrived at an extermination camp with hundreds of the deportees dead.

Deportations from Western Europe and from the Balkans proceeded somewhat differently. In the first stage the Jews scheduled for deportation were interned in transit camps in their native countries. After several weeks or even months, they were loaded onto trains headed for Poland. Travel conditions were better than those of Polish Jews and mortality en route was consequently lower. In some cases, Western Jews travelled in passenger cars, which only further nourished their illusion of being sent to work.

Upon the arrival of the transport at the extermination camp, the Jews were ordered to climb out. In the camps of Belzec, Sobibor and Treblinka, they were informed that they had arrived at a transit camp from which they would be sent to labor camps. Thereupon they were told to undress in preparation for a shower. Their clothes were to be disinfected. Women were told that their hair would have to be cut for sanitary reasons. Men would then be separated from women and children. Having undressed, the hapless and shocked victims were driven to the "showers" while being viciously beaten and terrorized. The "showers" turned out to be gas chambers. In Auschwitz, after disembarking onto the platform, a selection usually took place. Roughly 20% of the deportees — the young and able-bodied — would be picked out for work, their consignment to the gas chamber postponed for a time. At the same time, however, some transports did not go through any selection: all the victims, regardless of age or physical condition, were dispatched to the gas chambers upon arrival. On the other hand, in a few cases a whole transport was kept in the camp for some time before being gassed. The elaborate Nazi system of camouflage and deception kept the victims in a state of constant uncertainty as to their fate which ended only when they breathed their last in the gas chamber.

The German machinery of deportation worked with awesome efficiency. Millions of Jews went through the same trail of suffering which began at their homes and ended in the gas chamber of the death camp.

Poland, the Lodz district (Warthegau)

Killing of Jews from the Lodz district commenced with the establishment of the first extermination camp in Chelmno on December 8, 1941. In the aftermath of depor-

216. Warsaw ghetto: Jews receiving
bread ration prior to deportation.

tations to the areas of the General Government which lasted from the end of 1939 until the middle of 1940, there were still 250,000 Jews left in the district, including 150,00 in the Lodz ghetto. Over the period from mid-October to early November 1941, 20,000 additional Jews from the Reich and the Protectorate (Czechoslovakia) were brought to the Lodz ghetto, together with 5,000 Gypsies. They, too, were destined to be deported to their deaths. In the course of the deportations to Chelmno, which lasted until October 1942, nearly 150,000 people perished. Several thousand Jews were shot to death in the vicinity of their homes prior to and in the course of deportation to Chelmno. By the fall of 1942, all ghettos in the Lodz district were liquidated with the exception of the Lodz ghetto itself and several labor camps, where approximately 100,000 Jews still remained. Since the majority of the Lodz ghetto residents worked at enterprises of vital importance for the German war effort, the ghetto continued to exist for the next two years. With the Red Army approaching the area, the ghetto was finally liquidated in the second half of 1944. Its 60,000 remaining residents were sent to Auschwitz for extermination.

Poland, General Government

Deportations of the General Government Jews, whose number had been estimated at the Wannsee Conference at 2,284,000, commenced with the construction of the Belzec the extermination camp at Sobibor began functioning, and reached their climax with the establishment of the third extermination camp in the General Government — at Treblinka — on July 23, 1942. Only July 19, 1942, three days before the beginning of the great deportation from the Warsaw ghetto, Himmler issued an order requiring that the transfer of Jews from the Central Government to extermination camps be completed by December 31, 1942. After that date only a limited number of Jewish workers were to be left in "collection camps" located in some of the large cities of the General Government.

According to the deportation plan worked out by the staff of Operation Reinhard, the General Government was divided into three sectors. The Jews of the Lublin district, Eastern Galicia (Lvov), and Western Galicia (Krakow) were sent to the extermination camp of Belzec. With the establishment of the Sobibor camp, deportations of Jews from the Lublin district to this camp also began. The Jewish residents of Warsaw and the Warsaw district, as well as the Kielce and Radom districts, were deported to Treblinka. Over a short period of just two months, from its establishment until September 22, 1942, over 250,000 Jews from the Warsaw ghetto were murdered there. Deportees to these three camps included scores of thousands of German, Austrian and Czechoslovak Jews who had been deported previously to ghettos in the General Government, primarily to the Lublin district. In the course of these deportations thousands of Jews were shot to death in the vicinity of their places of residence.

By the winter of 1942, the majority of the Jewish inhabitants of the General Government had been murdered in various extermination camps. Owing to German demand for Jewish labor, Jewish workers were left in the Warsaw ghetto, as well as in a number of other ghettos and labor camps. The Warsaw ghetto was finally liquidated during the months of April/May 1943, with part of its residents sent to the labor camps at Poniatowo and Trawniki, and to the Majdanek concentration camp. Others were exterminated at Treblinka, or were killed inside Warsaw ghetto during the uprising that occurred there (see page 320).

By the middle of 1943, thousands still remaining in the ghettos and labor camps of Eastern Galicia had been shot near their homes. The remaining inhabitants of the Western Galicia ghettos were deported either to the extermination camp of Auschwitz or to the concentration camp at Plaszow.

Some 600,000 Jews were murdered in the Belzec camp, which continued to function until December 1942. In Treblinka, operative until the end of August 1943, 870,000 Jews were murdered. By October 14, 1943, when the Sobibor extermination camp halted its killing operations, some 250,000 Jews had perished there. Scores of thousands of Jews from other countries (see below) together with several thousand Gypsies also met their death in these camps.

Operation Harvest Festival (*Erntefest*), carried out on November 3, 1943, amounted to the last large-scale extermination campaign in the General Government. On that day 42,000 Jews, including women and children, inmates of the Poniatowo, Trawniki and Majdanek camps, were murdered.

The Jews of Upper Silesia (Zaglebie in Polish), which had been incorporated into the Reich, were deported to Auschwitz. Deportations, primarily from the cities of

Bedzin and Sosnowiec, were carried out from May through August 1942. The ultimate liquidation of the last Jews in this region took place in August 1943.

Poland, Generalbezirk (General District) Bialystok

The first wave of killings swept over the Bialystok district as early as July–September 1941, shortly after the German attack on the Soviet Union. The *Einsatzgruppen* murdered scores of thousands of Jews at that time. In mid-October 1942, deportations began to Treblinka and Auschwitz; they went on until mid-February 1943. During that time 180,000 Jews were exterminated, with 30,000 left behind in the Bialystok ghetto, which was finally liquidated in the second half of August 1943. Its residents were deported to Treblinka, Auschwitz and Majdanek.

*　　*　　*

Some 3.35 million Jews lived in Poland on the eve of World War II. About 3 million were murdered by the Nazis; over 350,000 survived. Of this total, close to 250,000 eluded the grasp of the Nazi machinery of destruction as refugees in the Soviet Union. The 100,000 to 120,000 Polish Jews who spent the war under Nazi rule and survived included camp survivors, as well as those who either hid with the aid of Poles, or lived as Aryans, or stayed in the forests and fought as partisans.

218

218. Krosniewice (near Kutno, Poland): a group of deported Jews en route to the death camps.

219. Wloclawek, Poland: deportation of Jews to the Chelmno death camp.

220. Deportation of Jews in Poland.

219

220

221. Siedlice, Poland: railway station with Jews aboard freight cars bound for the Treblinka death camp.

222. Siedlice, Poland: Jews shot to death at the railway station before they could board the train to Treblinka. The two photos were taken by an Austrian soldier, Hubert Ploch, who travelled to the Eastern front on August 21, 1942.

223. Lodz ghetto, Poland: deportation of Jews. Jewish policemen were forced to supervise the deportations.

221

222

223

224

224. Lodz ghetto, Poland: Jews being assembled prior to deportation to death camps.

225. Lodz ghetto, Poland: deportees boarding a train.

226. Lodz ghetto, Poland: deportation of Jewish children.

225

226

227

227. Deportation from Lodz.

228, 229. Grodno, Generalbezirk
Byalistok, Poland: deportation of Jews
to the Treblinka and Auschwitz death
camps.

222

231

230. Warsaw ghetto: deportation of Jewish children.

231. Jews being ferried to death camps in open cattle cars.

232. Janusz Korczak and children in the Warsaw ghetto prior to deportation.

Deportations of German, Austrian and Czechoslovak (Protectorate) Jews

Deportations of Jews from Germany, Austria and Czechoslovakia (the Protectorate of Bohemia and Moravia) were carried out in accordance with a uniform and comprehensive plan. The first wave of deportations destined for the ghettos in the General Government swept over the Jews of these countries from the end of 1939 to the middle of 1940. As a preliminary measure prior to the second wave of deportations, all Reich Jews over age 6 were required to wear an identifying badge in the shape of a yellow Star of David, beginning on September 19, 1941. On October 23, 1941, a decree was promulgated prohibiting the emigration of Jews from the Reich. Deportations to extermination camps began in October 1941, when 20,000 Jews were transferred to the Lodz ghetto and from there to the extermination camp at Chelmno. At about the same time, top SS leaders determined that the occupied Soviet areas offered better opportunities for stepped-up killing operations that those present in Lodz. Beginning in November 1941, transports with about 1,000 Jews each started arriving in the Nazi-occupied Soviet zone — Kovno, Riga and Minsk — where *Einsatzgruppen* were active. Some of these deportees were killed immediately upon arrival; others joined the residents of the Minsk and Riga ghettos and perished together with them during the liquidation. Deportations to the occupied Soviet zone went on until the end of 1942.

The "ghetto" of Theresienstadt

This ghetto, set up in an old fortress town in Czechoslovakia, was a showpiece of the Nazi campaign of deception designed to camouflage the real purpose of the "final solution." As a "model camp," purporting to provide the deported Jews with relatively comfortable living conditions, it was meant to deceive the Jews, world public opinion, and representatives of the International Red Cross. Jewish inmates of Theresienstadt pursued a whole range of cultural activities: orchestras gave concerts, theater companies staged plays, sport and painting competitions took place, etc. The inmates comprised elderly Jews from Germany, war invalids, decorated World War I veterans, as well as Jews with important Aryan relatives. In practice, Theresienstadt served as a stopping place for Jews before their final destination in the Nazi-occupied Soviet zone or at Auschwitz and Treblinka.

Beginning in November 1941, over 73,000 Czechoslovak Jews were deported to Theresienstadt. Fifty-eight thousand arrived there from the Reich and another 8,000 from other countries. Altogether some 140,000 Jews passed through Theresienstadt. Slightly over 17,000 were left on the day of liberation in early May 1945.

Certain transports of Jews from the Third Reich went straight to Auschwitz without passing through Theresienstadt. Of the total of over half a million German Jews living in the country on the eve of the Nazi takeover, 200,000 perished in the

"Final Solution." A majority of the survivors emigrated from Germany before the gates were shut. A few thousand eluded death within Germany with the help of local inhabitants.

There were 185,000 Jews in Austria on the eve of the *Anschluss*. About 65,000 of them were murdered; others managed to emigrate. Of the 118,000 Jews in the Protectorate of Bohemia and Moravia (Czechoslovakia), 75,000 to 80,000 were exterminated. The rest survived through emigration.

233

234

233. Würzburg, Germany: deportation
of Jews, 1942.

234. Wiesbaden, Germany: deportation
of Jews, 1942.

235. Regensburg, Germany: deportation of Jews, 1942.

236. Plzen (Pilsen), Czechoslovakia: deportation of Jews.

Slovakia

On the eve of the German occupation, about 137,000 Jews lived in Slovakia, of whom 40,000 lived in the southeastern part of the country ceded, on Hungarian request and under German pressure, to Hungary at the end of 1938. The deportation of the remaining 90,000 Slovakian Jews was carried out in two stages: the first lasted from March to October 1942, and the second from October 1944 until March 1945.

The government of Slovakia collaborated with the Germans in deporting the local Jews. It even pledged to pay Germany 500 marks for each deported Jew. In the first stage, 57,000 Jews were deported to Auschwitz and the Lublin district. Those deported to Lublin perished in the death camps of Belzec, Sobibor and Treblinka.

In late 1942 several Slovakian Jewish leaders set up an underground "working group" which endeavored to rouse Jewish and non-Jewish public opinion in the world against the mass extermination of Jews. Members of this group succeeded in establishing ties with Jewish bodies abroad and informing them of the situation in the country. They also contacted Wisliceny of the SS who was in charge of organizing the deportation of Jews from Slovakia. Offering promises of financial reward, they attempted to prevail upon him, and indirectly on his superiors in Berlin, to postpone the deportations of European Jews to the death camps. The venture, later called the "European Plan," came to grief. Similarly, some Vatican attempts to intervene with the Slovak government — headed by a Catholic priest, Father Josef Tiso — to prevent the deportations, bore no fruit.

The second stage of the deportations came in the aftermath of an uprising which broke out in Slovakia in August–October 1944. The uprising, in which many Jews participated, was suppressed. Four volunteers who had been flown from the Land of Israel and dropped by parachute, joined the uprising and died in combat. Of some 10,000 Jews who took part in the uprising or lived in the areas controlled by the resisters, over 2,000 were murdered by the Germans and Slovak collaborators during the suppression of the revolt. Others were sent to concentration camps. From October 1944 until March 1945, about 13,500 Jews were sent to Auschwitz. After the discontinuation of killings in Auschwitz in October 1944, Slovak Jews were sent to concentration camps in Germany and to Theresienstadt. Some of them survived. About 5,000 Jews who were hiding in Slovakia eluded the deportations. Those Slovak Jews who lived in the territory annexed by Hungary shared the fate of Hungarian Jews who were deported to Auschwitz in the first half of 1944 (see below). Of the 90,000 Jews living in "independent" Slovakia, about 70,000 were murdered. Together with the Jews in the territory incorporated into Hungary, the number of Slovak Jews exterminated by the Nazis reached some 110,000, out of a Jewish population of 137,000 in prewar Slovakia.

237

237. Slovakia: Jews boarding trains to
the death camps in the Lublin area and
to Auschwitz, March–October 1942.

238. Slovakia: deportation of Jews (exact
location unknown).

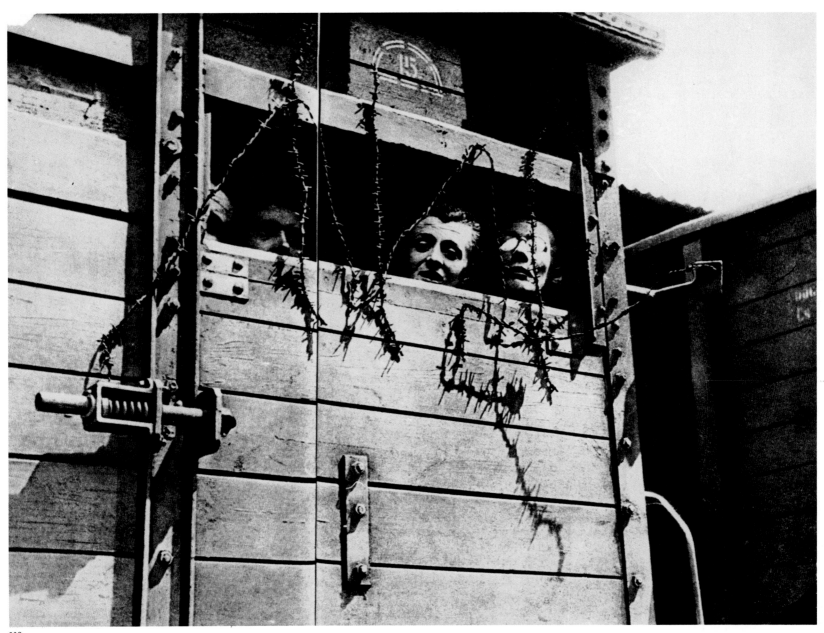

239

239. Women in cattle cars en route to
the death camps.

240. Aristide de Souza Mendes,
Portuguese Consul-General in Bordeaux,
France.

France

In the aftermath of the French surrender, a great many Jews living in the German occupied zone moved to Southern France, controlled by the Vichy government. About 195,000 Jews, out of a total Jewish population of 350,000, were concentrated there. The remainder found themselves under direct Nazi rule.

From May to December 1941, the French police and gendarmerie rounded up thousands of Jews in Paris and its environs. The primary targets were Jews lacking French nationality. Most of the detainees were interned at Drancy, near Paris.

In early summer 1942, preparations began toward deporting the Jews of France, Belgium and Holland to death camps in Poland. On June 11, 1942, Eichmann held a meeting with his representatives in the three countries for the purpose of coordinating deportation plans. The Drancy camp was designated as an assembly point for French Jews subject to deportation. According to the agreement concluded between the SS and the Vichy government, the first to be deported were Jews who had arrived in France as refugees as well as foreign nationals. The task of rounding up the candidates for deportation was assigned to the French police. Deportations began in the occupied zone, but later on Jews from the unoccupied zone were included. Transports of one thousand Jews each left Drancy for Auschwitz and Sobibor. From July 19 to the end of September 1942, 22 such transports departed from France. With the German occupation of the hitherto unoccupied zone in November 1942, local Jews were also shipped off to Poland. Thousands of Jews fled from southern France to the Italian-occupied French city of Nice and to Spain. The Portugese Consul in Bordeaux, Aristides de Souza Mendes, assisted them greatly in reaching Portugal, against the explicit orders of his government. In September 1943, the Germans occupied Nice too. Deportations of Jews from there inevitably followed.

240

Altogether, over 75,000 Jews from France were murdered. Thousands, including children, eluded deportation by hiding, or smuggling themselves across the border into Switzerland and Spain. Underground Jewish organizations undertook rescue activities with the help of the French underground.

In the French colonies of Algeria, Tunisia and Morocco, Vichy authorities promulgated anti-Jewish policies which included sending local Jews to labor camps set up in these countries. They also undertook preparations for deportation to death camps in Europe. Developments on the war fronts, together with the liberation of North Africa, followed by the liberation of France, frustrated German plans to exterminate most French and North African Jews.

Belgium

In the fall of 1941, German occupation authorities took a series of measures against the Jews, laying the groundwork for deportation. In October 1941, Jews were forbidden to travel outside the four major cities: Antwerp, Brussels, Liège and Charleroi. On June 6, 1942 they were forced to wear Star of David armbands.

In the summer of 1942, deportations began. Transports of 1,000 people each left for Auschwitz via the transit camp at Malines, which served as an assembly point. The first transport left Malines in early August 1942, and the deportations continued through late July 1944.

The Jewish population of Belgium on the eve of the German invasion was roughly 90,000. Some 40,000 were sent to their deaths in the extermination camps in Poland. Some 25,000 fled to France, only to join the ranks of deportees from that country. The remainder succeeded in finding refuge in Belgium with the help of both the local Belgian and Jewish undergrounds, as well as protection extended by individuals.

The Netherlands

As early as 1941 the Germans seized several hundred young Dutch Jews, who were eventually deported to the concentration camp at Mauthausen in Austria, where they met their deaths. In January 1942, over five thousand Dutch Jews were placed in forced labor camps set up in Holland. Preparations for deportation included a series of measures such as the concentration of Jews from outlying districts in Amsterdam, introduction of the identifying yellow armband in April 1942, and other steps. Two transit camps were set up, a large one at Westerbork and a smaller one at Vught, where Jews were concentrated prior to their transport to Auschwitz.

Transports to death camps began in mid-July 1942. Each transport consisted of 1,000 to 2,000 Jews. Altogether, 67 trains with 60,000 Jews on them left for Auschwitz, most of them in 1942. Nineteen trains with 34,000 Jews went to Sobibor between March and July 1943. Six trains carrying nearly 5,000 Jews left for Theresienstadt; 4,000 more Jews were sent to Bergen-Belsen and Ravensbrueck. Nearly all the deportations were carried out over a 15-month period, beginning in July 1942 and continuing through September 1943. The last train for Auschwitz left the transit camp at Westerbork on September 7, 1944.

Thousands of Dutch Jews disobeyed the deportation orders and went into hiding with the active assistance of the local population. Some of them were caught and sent to the camps; others succeeded in saving themselves. Out of a Jewish population of 140,000, including some 30,000 refugees from Germany and Austria living in the Netherlands on the eve of the Nazi invasion, some 105,000 perished.

Luxembourg

On the eve of the war, some 3,000 Jews lived in the Grand Duchy of Luxembourg. About two-thirds of them succeeded in fleeing the country shortly after the occupation. Most went to the unoccupied French zone; others managed to reach Spain and Portugal. About 800 Luxembourgian Jews were deported to death camps in Poland where they perished. After the liberation several hundred Jews were found to have survived in Luxembourg.

241. Amsterdam: Anna Frank.

242. Amsterdam: deportation of Jews to Westerbork camp.

241

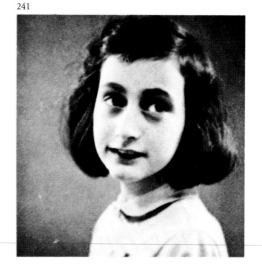

242

235

243

244

236

245

243. Westerbork, Holland: arrival of
Jews from Amsterdam.

244. Jews from Westerbork boarding
cattle trucks bound for the Auschwitz
and Sobibor death camps.

245. Westerbork, Holland: a Jewish girl
peering from a freight car en route to a
death camp in Poland.

Norway

A small Jewish community of about 1,800 existed in Norway before the war. After its occupation Norway became a Reich Commissariat, ruled by a local government headed by Vidkun Quisling (hence the derogatory designation of collaborators as "quislings"). Until the latter part of 1942, Norwegian Jews lived relatively undisturbed. However, in November 1942, the Jews were concentrated in Oslo and deportations began on November 26. One boatload of victims was dispatched by sea from Oslo to the German city of Stettin; they were subsequently sent to Auschwitz. Quisling and his men collaborated fully in the operation. Altogether about 760 Jews were deported. Some 900 managed to evade deportation and internment camps by crossing the border to Sweden with the assistance of the Norwegian underground.

Denmark

Having surrendered to the German ultimatum in April 1940, Denmark retained its independence *de jure*. The king remained on the throne and the Danish governing institutions remained intact. Danish authorities resisted German demands to institute measures against its 8,000 Jews.

Even the restricted independence of Denmark was not to the Nazis' liking and in August 1943, the German army entered Copenhagen, disarmed the Danish army, imprisoned the king, and took over the governance of the country. At the same time, however, local administration remained in Danish hands. With the changed political situation, the Germans were determined to deport the Danish Jews to the extermination camps in Poland. Deportation plans were revealed to F. Duckwitz, a German who served as maritime attaché at the German mission in Copenhagen. He reported this plan to Danish Social Democratic leaders. Forewarned of the impending deportation, Danish Jews went into hiding with the active assistance of the whole population. In a roundup carried out by the Germans on the night of October 1–2, 1943, only a few hundred Jews were caught. In an extraordinary operation carried out by the Danish underground, some 7,200 Jews were hidden and then ferried across to Sweden with the consent of the Swedish government.

Nearly 500 Jews whom the Germans managed to round up were sent to Theresienstadt instead of Auschwitz. The Danish authorities persisted in inquiring about their fate. Delegates from the Danish Red Cross visited Theresienstadt and made efforts on their behalf. In April 1945 the Danish Jews were returned to their country from Theresienstadt.

246. Danish boat rescuing Jews.

Finland

Despite its alliance with Germany in the war against the Soviet Union, Finnish governing circles, headed by Marshal Mannerheim, refused to accede to Himmler's demand to deport local Jews to death camps in Poland. Two thousand Finnish Jews survived the war.

Italy

As the principal ally of Nazi Germany, Italy decreed various restrictions and other measures upon its 57,000 Jews who lived in the country prior to World War II. At the same time, however, the situation of Italian Jews was enviable compared with that of Jews in other European countries allied with Germany. The Italian government refused to give in to German demands concerning deportations to the death camps. With the Allied invasion of Southern Italy and the Italian surrender in early September 1943, the situation of the Jews in that country worsened. The Germans responded by occupying Northern and Central Italy, including Rome. Some 35,000 Italian Jews found themselves under direct Nazi rule.

On October 16, 1943, the Jews of Rome were rounded up and more than one thousand of them were sent to Auschwitz. In November, other Italian cities were swept by the deportations operation. Special internment camps for Jews awaiting transport to Auschwitz were set up in the north. However, despite German efforts in this direction, a majority of Italian Jews managed to evade deportation by finding refuge with the friendly Italian population. Hundreds of Jews joined the Italian partisans. Altogether, some 7,500 Italian Jews were sent to the extermination camps and perished there.

Romania

Mass murder of Romanian Jews began one week after the German onslaught against the Soviet Union, in which Romanian forces took an active part. On June 29–30, 1941, Romanian troops organized a mass pogrom in the town of Jassy in which some 10,000 Jews lost their lives. With the occupation of Bessarabia and Northern Bukovina by the Germans and Romanians, the local Jews were incarcerated in ghettos. The *Einsatzgruppen* and Romanian troops carried out mass executions in the area. The number of Jews murdered at this time is estimated at 150,000. As the slaughter continued and for some time thereafter mass deportations of Jews from these areas to Transnistria took place.

Before the war some 300,000 Jews lived in the area of Transnistria, later annexed by Romania, with 180,000 living in the city of Odessa. Thousands upon thousands were executed by *Einsatzgruppe* D assigned to this region. Romanian units, together with Ukrainian and "Volksdeutsche" volunteers, completed the job of murder. When on October 16, 1941, the city of Odessa was occupied following a siege, about 90,000 Jews remained there. Others had been evacuated or fled across the sea during the siege. Six days after the occupation, an enormous explosion reduced the building of the Romanian army headquarters to rubble. Dozens of Romanian military personnel and Germans were killed. Romanian gendarmes reacted to the bombing by murdering 35,000 Jews within a few days. Within the next several months, the remaining Odessa Jews were deported to camps located in Transnistria where they met their deaths.

Transnistria served as a dumping ground for some 150,000 Jews expelled from Bessarabia and Northern Bukovina, together with a few thousand more from central

Romania. They were incarcerated in various ghettos and camps. Remnants of the local Jews joined the Romanian Jews who had been driven out to Transnistria. The terrible conditions prevailing there, including hunger and disease, took the lives of 90,000 of the deportees. Romanian Jews who had stayed behind rendered some assistance to their deported brethren in Transnistria, which somewhat alleviated their situation.

In early 1943, the ruling Romanian circles realized that the tide of war was turning against Germany. They responded by mitigating their anti-Jewish policies and the situation of Jews in the country slightly improved. Furthermore, Romania refused to deport its Jews to death camps in Poland. For its part, the local Jewish leadership undertook various rescue activities and even succeeded in bringing back to the country several thousand of the Transnistrian deportees, mostly children.

Some 164,000 Jews lived in Northern Transylvania, which had been ceded to Hungary. In April and May 1944, the process of their ghettoization commenced. By late May–early June, 1944, Jews from Northern Transylvania, together with Hungarian Jews, were deported to Auschwitz. About 125,000 of them perished. Out of a Jewish population of 750,000 in prewar Romania, 350,000 lost their lives in the Holocaust.

Yugoslavia

With the occupation of the country in April 1941, Yugoslavia was partitioned among Germany and its allies: Italy, Bulgaria, Hungary and the puppet state of Croatia. The fate of the Jews in each of the partition areas was determined by the policies of the occupying country.

Of 12,000 Jews in prewar Serbia, over two-thirds lived in the capital city of Belgrade. In August 1941, the German army interned 5,000 adult male Jews in camps set up in Serbia. By mid-November all of them had been shot to death. By May 1942, all the women and children had also been massacred. In the murder of Serbian Jews, the Germans used gas vans, along with other methods.

Some 40,000 Jews lived in Croatia on the eve of the war. Many of them were interned in concentration camps in Croatia by the local authorities. By the spring of 1943, most of the Jews had been murdered by Croatian nationalists called Ustashi. About 5,000 Jews were sent to Auschwitz. The situation of Jews living in the Adriatic coastal area occupied by the Italian army was enviable compared with that of Jews in other areas of Yugoslavia. In fact, thousands of them survived the Holocaust.

Over 7,000 Jews lived in parts of Macedonia annexed by Bulgaria. As they were not Bulgarian nationals, the authorities turned them over to the Germans who sent them to Treblinka where they were murdered in March 1943. Some 25,000 Jews who lived in the Backa basin incorporated into Hungary, shared the fate of other Hungarian Jews. Several thousand were murdered in Backa; others were deported to Auschwitz in the early summer of 1944 and murdered there.

Almost from the outset of the occupation, a widely-based partisan movement led by Josip Broz Tito developed in Yugoslavia. Several thousand Jews fought in the ranks of the partisans during the war.

Of the 75,000 Jews living in the country before the war, about 60,000 perished in the Holocaust.

Greece

Following the occupation of Greece by Germany and Italy in March 1941, the country was divided up into three occupation zones. The southern and central parts of the country, including Athens, were under the Italians. Germany occupied Northern Greece, including the city of Salonika where 56,000 Jews lived. Because of the cultural and economic strength of its Jewish community, Salonika was called the "Jerusalem of Greece." Western Thrace in the northeastern part of the country was awarded to Bulgaria.

The first to feel the brunt of anti-Jewish measures were the Jews living under German rule in the city of Salonika and its environs, including several islands in the Aegean Sea. Ghettoization took place at a later time, in February 1943. At the same time the local Jews were ordered to wear Star of David badges. As in other places, these steps preceded deportations to death camps.

Deportations to Auschwitz began in mid-March 1943 and continued through mid-August of the same year. By that time about 49,900 Jews were deported. A few thousand Jews managed to flee to the Italian occupation zone. More than 4,200 Jews living in the area annexed by Bulgaria were turned over by Bulgarian authorities to the Germans, who subsequently deported them to Treblinka in March 1943.

Until September 1943, when, following the surrender of Italy to the Allies, the whole of Greece came under German military rule, Jews living in the Italian occupation zone remained relatively undisturbed. Early in April 1944, some 5,200 Jews from Athens and other communities were deported to Auschwitz. Some 6,000 managed to escape deportation by hiding in the mountains or finding refuge among the local population. The Greek underground helped the Jews to find refuge and some of them fought in the ranks of the Greek partisans.

The last to be deported were Jews living on the islands of Corfu, Crete and Rhodes. Some 1,800 Jews were rounded up in Corfu, 1,200 in Rhodes and 200 in Crete. In the months of June–July 1944, all of them were sent to Auschwitz and only a handful survived.

Of the original population of 77,000, over 60,000 Greek Jews were annihilated in the Holocaust, most of them in Auschwitz.

Bulgaria

About 50,000 Jews lived in prewar Bulgaria. Although neutral at the outbreak of the war in September 1939, Bulgaria joined the Axis in March 1941 and German troops were stationed in the country. In return for its alliance with Germany, and following the occupation of Greece by the Germans and Italians, Western Thrace, belonging to Greece, together with Yugoslavian parts of Macedonia, were awarded to her. Nearly 14,000 Jews lived in these areas.

Bulgarian government began introducing anti-Jewish measures. A special tax on Jewish-owned property was enacted, various economic restrictions instituted, and forced labor in camps set up in the countryside was introduced. The Star of David was introduced in September 1943. It should be noted, however, that these measures were not strictly observed and the situation of Bulgarian Jews was good compared with that of Jews in other European countries. In the second half of 1942 and early 1943, the Germans exerted growing pressure on Bulgaria to deport its Jews to the death camps. Circles in Parliament, the Bulgarian Orthodox Church, the Royal Court, and sections of public opinion in the country expressed their opposition to deportation of the Jews. Their counterpressure led the Bulgarian government to refuse to turn over its Jewish nationals to the Germans. At the same time, however, the deportation of the Macedonian and Thracian Jews remained in force. Nearly 11,500 Jews living in these areas, recently annexed by Bulgaria, were rounded up by the local authorities, interned in camps, and turned over to the Germans. They were deported to the extermination camp of Treblinka in March and early April 1943. In May 1943, the Bulgarian government ordered the dispersal to provincial towns of nearly 20,000 Jews living in the capital city of Sofia. The resettlement was carried out at the end of May and early June 1943. With the exception of Jews in the areas annexed by Bulgaria, Bulgarian Jewry survived the Holocaust.

247

247. Aboard a deportation ship on the Danube carrying Jews from Thrace and Macedonia to Treblinka.

248. Macedonia: deportation of Jews, March, 1943.

248

Hungary

Hungary entered into an alliance with Germany as early as 1938. With the occupation of Czechoslovakia by Germany, Hungary was rewarded with parts of Slovakia and Subcarpathian Ukraine, which it annexed. In 1940, with German help, Northern Transylvania was ceded from Romania to Hungary. Following the occupation of Yugoslavia, Hungary occupied the northeastern parts of that country.

As a result of these territorial additions, about 275,000 Jews found themselves under Hungarian rule, together with the original Jewish population of 450,000. A census conducted in 1941 put the total Jewish population in the country at 725,000. In addition to this number, there were tens of thousands of converts and offspring of mixed marriages who were considered as Jews under the Nazi racial laws.

Notwithstanding anti-Jewish enactments and other restrictions imposed against Jews as early as 1938–1939, their situation was relatively good. This is demonstrated by the fact that thousands of Jewish refugees from Germany, Austria, Czechoslovakia and Poland chose to flee to Hungary. The situation took a turn for the worse with the German attack against the Soviet Union, in which some Hungarian troops took part.

In August 1941, the Hungarian government rounded up 18,500 Jews, mostly foreign nationals in its annexed territories, and expelled them acros the border to Kamenets-Podolsk in the German-occupied Ukraine. The *Einsatzgruppen* active in this area massacred 14,000 of the deportees. Several thousand Yugoslav Jews were murdered by the Hungarian occupation forces at Novi Sad, shortly after their entry into the areas annexed by Hungary from Yugoslavia. Scores of thousands of Jews were conscripted into forced-labor battalions placed under the jurisdiction of the Hungarian army; they were put to work just behind the front lines in the occupied areas of the Soviet Union. Thousands of them died of overwork, hunger and disease.

After the first wave of massacres in 1941, a period of relative calm set in for Hungarian Jews which lasted several years. However, political and military developments, compounded by the fear of Hungary signing a separate truce with the Allies, induced Germany to occupy the country on March 19, 1944. The occupation drastically changed the situation of Hungarian Jewry. On the same day, Eichmann arrived in Budapest and his staff began preparations for the deportation of Hungarian Jews to Auschwitz. Ghettoization inevitably followed and the yellow Star of David was introduced. Deportations to the death camps were carried out from May 15 through July 8, 1944. During that time, 445,000 Jews from provincial towns, as well as from the annexed territories, were sent to Auschwitz. The operation was carried out by the Hungarian police and troops of the indigenous fascist organization, the Arrow-Cross.

In the meantime, the Rescue and Relief Committee established by Hungarian Jews in the first years of the war to aid refugees who had arrived in the country maintained clandestine contacts with Jewish organizations abroad. It relayed information about the events in Hungary and called for action to halt the deportations. Furthermore, the Committee contacted SS officers in charge of the deportations and

249

250

249–251. Tens of thousands of Jews in Hungary were saved thanks to the activities of the Swedish diplomat Raul Wallenberg (249), the Red Cross representative, Friedrich Born (250) and the Swiss Consul in Budapest, Karl Lutz (251).

252. Budapest: round-up of Jewish intelligentsia, spring, 1944.

251

252

began negotiations aimed at delaying them. At that time the Red Army was approaching Hungary and it was clear that liberation was only a few months away. Consequently, the main task was to gain time. Himmler's representatives offered to ransom Hungarian Jews in exchange for trucks to be supplied to Germany by the Allies. Although nothing substantial came out of these negotiations, the deportations were discontinued for some time.

With the resumption of deportations in November 1944, it became the turn of the Jews of Budapest. Since Auschwitz was then being liquidated and other extermination camps in occupied Poland no longer functioned, Germany became the destination for the deported Jews. As railroad transportation was unavailable, it was decided to march the deportees to the Austrian border. On November 8, 1944, in cold and rain, scores of thousands of Jews set off on foot from Budapest to the Austrian border, a distance of nearly 200 kilometers. Many of them died en route. The survivors were put to work building fortifications, or were incarcerated in Dachau and Mathhausen. Thousands of Jews were saved from deportation thanks to the activities of Swedish diplomat Raul Wallenberg, Swiss Consul Karl Lutz and Friedrich Born, IRCR (Red Cross) representative stationed in Budapest. They supplied Hungarian Jews with "protection passports" and placed them into special protected houses.

In December 1944, the Soviet army reached the outskirts of Budapest and the city, including the ghetto with over 100,000 Jews, was liberated on January 6, 1945. Of the 450,000 Jews of pre-1938 Hungary, about 300,000 perished.

Hungarian Jews were the last Jewish community in Europe to be destroyed by the Nazi destruction machine. Military developments, especially the defeats suffered by Nazi Germany in the last phases of the war, prevented the deportation and annihilation of the Jews still remaining in several European countries.

253. Szombathely, Hungary: deportation of Jews.

254. Round-up of Jews from small villages in Hungary for deportation to Poland.

255. Hungary: Jews awaiting deportation at the railway station.

253

256

257

258

256, 257. Hungarian Jews in the ghetto.

258. Budapest: round-up of Jewish girls,
autumn, 1944.

Plunder of Jewish property

The persecution of Jews in Nazi-occupied Europe and their deportation to the death camps involved the expropriation and outright plunder of Jewish property in truly gigantic proportions. The value of property seized by the Nazis is estimated at billions of dollars. Anti-Jewish statutes enacted in various countries legalized vast expropriations and seizures. The requisitioned Jewish-owned real estate included apartments, industrial enterprises, businesses, land, etc. The Nazis also gained control of bank accounts, cash, securities, bonds and more. Whatever was not plundered through legislation was left behind by Jews deported to ghettos and death camps. In the death camps themselves, immense wealth accumulated from various belongings, valuables and money which the deportees had taken with them, acting in the belief they were being resettled. The Nazi henchmen even removed gold fillings from the teeth of the murdered victims. Part of this wealth went directly to the German authorities; the remainder was appropriated by the local governing agencies in each country, city and town. Various German and non-German bodies fought over the right to Jewish-owned property. A sizable portion of it fell into the hands of the indigenous population, sometimes close or distant neighbors of the victims. The SS and local police detachments directly involved in driving the Jews out of their homes, guards escorting the transports, and staff of the death camps also obtained their share. Property that had been accumulated through the labor and great effort of generations was taken away from its rightful owners over a period of just a few years.

Nazi Germany profited in yet another way from its persecution of Jews: in the exploitation of their labor. Hundreds of thousands of Jews working at forced labor in ghettos, camps, labor battalions and German factories provided an inexhaustible source of practically free labor. Both German state-controlled enterprises and private firms reaped huge benefits from it. The exploitation of Jews lasted until they were completely worn out by overwork and died en masse of hunger, cold, disease and fatigue.

Thus it came to pass that the words with which God commanded the prophet Elijah the Tishbite to rebuke Ahab: "Hast thou killed and also taken possession?" were fulfilled in the Holocaust.

THE DEATH CAMPS

The following photographs were taken by two SS men in Auschwitz-Birkenau: SS Unteroffizier Bernard Walter, head of the Identification Office, and his assistant Ernst Hoffmann. The photographs show the transport of Jews from the ghettos in Carpatho-Ruthenia, which was annexed by Hungary from Czechoslovakia in 1939. Taking photographs within the Auschwitz-Birkenau extermination camp (as in other camps) was strictly forbidden. In this case, however, a special permit was issued. The album of photographs was discovered in the Dora Nordhausen concentration camp shortly after liberation in 1945 by Mrs. Lilly Jacobs, a former Auschwitz prisoner.

259. A transport of Jews on arrival in the camp.

260

260. A train arriving at the loading platform in Auschwitz-Birkenau. Jews are still locked inside the sealed cars.

261. Auschwitz-Birkenau: disembarking from the train. The chimneys of crematorium no. 2 on the left and no. 3 on the right are visible in the distance.

262. Disembarking from the train in Auschwitz-Birkenau.

261

262

263. Auschwitz-Birkenau: disembarkation.

264. Auschwitz-Birkenau: disembarkation.

265. Auschwitz-Birkenau: selection. The Jews were first ordered to assemble in two groups, one of women and children, the other of men. Those physically fit were then sent to slave labor (about 10–15% of the total number). The rest went straight to the gas chambers (overleaf).

266. Women and children before selection.

267. Women selected for slave labor.

268

268. In the foreground: mothers and babies.

269. Auschwitz-Birkenau: loading platform during selection. The newly arrived deportees were ordered to line up in rows of five. None as yet realized what lay in store for them. Most believed that they had arrived in a labor or transit camp.

270. SS physician examining male arrivals. On the right — women who arrived with the same transport.

269

271. Auschwitz-Birkenau: selection.

272. Auschwitz-Birkenau: men after
being selected for slave labor in the camp.

273. Auschwitz-Birkenau: after being selected for slave labor, women had their hair shaved off.

276

274, 275, 276. Auschwitz-Birkenau:
women on their way to slave labor.

277

279

281

283

285

286

287

287, 288. Men and women sorting out belongings of those sent to gas chambers.

288

289. Old men waiting to be gassed (overleaf).

290. Men, women and children waiting in a grove
before being sent to the gas chambers (pp. 284–285).

AUSCHWITZ II BIRKENAU
EXTERMINATION CAMP

SS BARRACKS AND HQ.

CONVOYS

CONVOYS

NEW RAIL SPUR

WITZ I

291

286

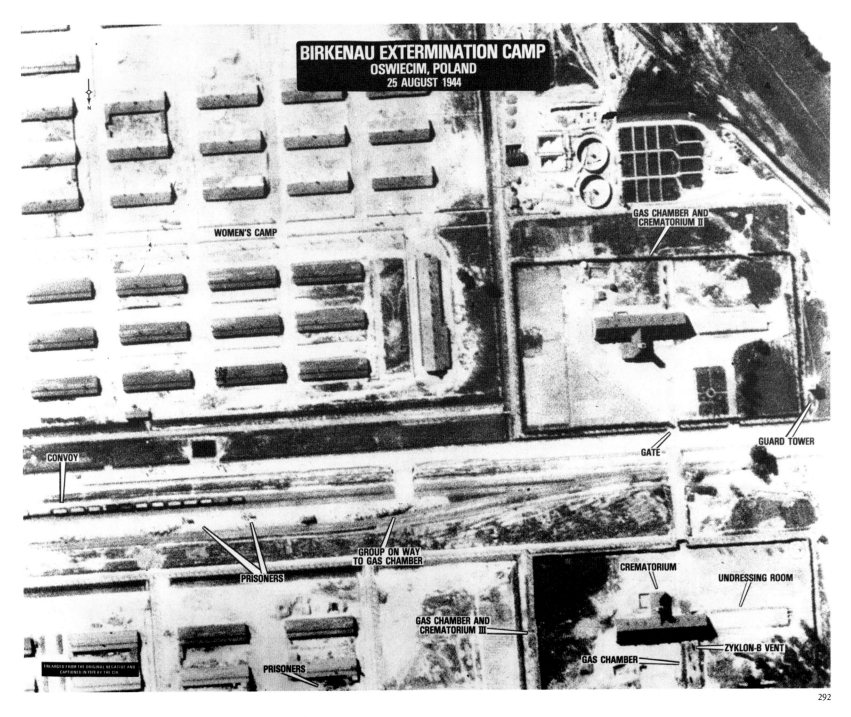

Within the image:

BIRKENAU EXTERMINATION CAMP
OSWIECIM, POLAND
25 AUGUST 1944

N

WOMEN'S CAMP

GAS CHAMBER AND
CREMATORIUM II

GATE

GUARD TOWER

CONVOY

GROUP ON WAY
TO GAS CHAMBER

PRISONERS

CREMATORIUM

UNDRESSING ROOM

GAS CHAMBER AND
CREMATORIUM III

ZYKLON-B VENT

GAS CHAMBER

PRISONERS

ENLARGED FROM THE ORIGINAL NEGATIVE AND
CAPTIONED IN 1978 BY THE CIA

292

291. Aerial view of Auschwitz-Birkenau.

292. Detail of the aerial view of
Auschwitz-Birkenau.

THE PLAN OF AUSCHWITZ II (BIRKENAU)
Late October 1944

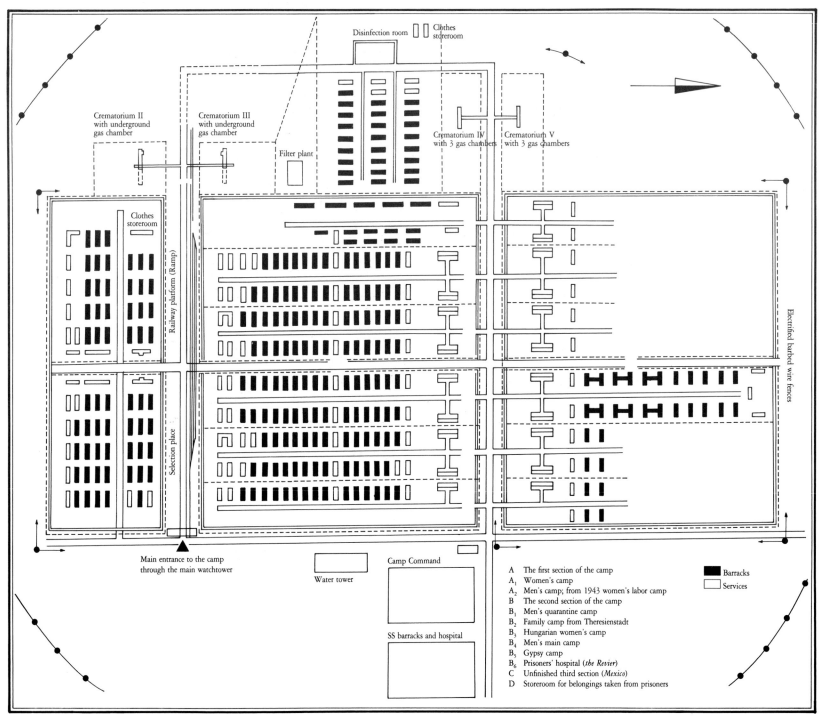

Disinfection room   Clothes storeroom

Crematorium II with underground gas chamber

Crematorium III with underground gas chamber

Filter plant

Crematorium IV with 3 gas chambers   Crematorium V with 3 gas chambers

Clothes storeroom

Railway platform (Ramp)

Selection place

Electrified barbed wire fences

Main entrance to the camp through the main watchtower

Water tower

Camp Command

SS barracks and hospital

A	The first section of the camp
A_1	Women's camp
A_2	Men's camp; from 1943 women's labor camp
B	The second section of the camp
B_1	Men's quarantine camp
B_2	Family camp from Theresienstadt
B_3	Hungarian women's camp
B_4	Men's main camp
B_5	Gypsy camp
B_6	Prisoners' hospital (the Revier)
C	Unfinished third section (Mexico)
D	Storeroom for belongings taken from prisoners

■ Barracks
□ Services

This plan is based on *The Death Factory — Document on Auschwitz* by Ota Kraus and Erich Kulka

293. A prisoner commits suicide by
running into the electrified barbed-wire
fence.

294, 295. Two of seven photographs taken clandestinely in Birkenau by a Sonderkommando worker (only three could be developed). The photos were smuggled out of Birkenau by the camp underground in order to alert the world to what was happening in the camps.

294. Naked Jewish women on their way to a gas chamber nicknamed the "bunker".

295. Burning of corpses gassed in the "bunker." The thousands of Jews who arrived from Hungary exceeded the capacity of the four crematoria in Birkenau and bodies were burned in open pits.

295

296. Ruins of gas chamber no. 2.

297. Ruins of the entrance to the
undressing room of gas chamber no. 2.

THE SOBIBOR DEATH CAMP

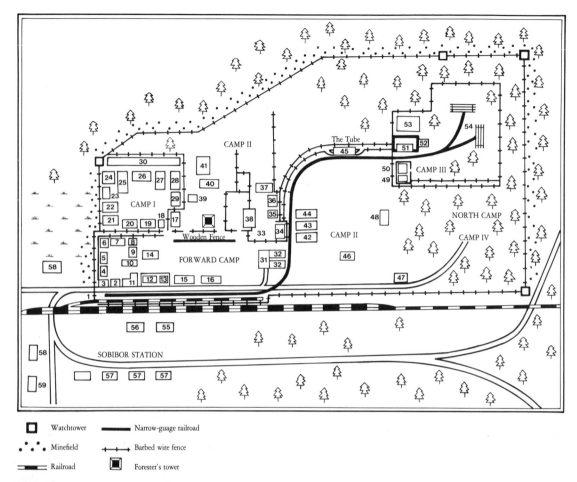

Forward Camp
1. Unloading platform
2. Dentist and jail for Ukrainian guards
3. Guard home
4. SS clothing store
5. SS quarters
6. SS quarters
7. Laundry
8. Well
9. Showers and barbershop for SS
10. Garage
11. SS kitchen and canteen
12. Living quarters of the camp commanders
13. Armory
14. Barracks for Ukrainian guards
15. Barracks for Ukrainian guards
16. Barracks for Ukrainian guards
17. Bakery

Camp I
18. Dispensary
19. Tailor shop for SS
20. Shoemaker and saddler shop for SS
21. Smithery
22. Carpentry
23. Latrine
24. Painters' shop
25. Barracks for male prisoners
26. Barracks for male prisoners
27. Prisoners' kitchen
28. Barracks for female prisoners
29. Shoemaker shop for Ukrainian guards
30. Water ditch

Camp II
31. Undressing barracks where deportees deposited their clothing and luggage
32. Barracks where luggage was sorted and stored
33. Undressing yard
34. Storage warehouse for food brought by the deportees
35. Electrical generator
36. Storage of silverware
37. Stable and barns
38. Administration building and storeroom for valuables
39. SS ironing room
40. Shoe warehouse
41. Garden
42. Barracks for storing property
43. Barracks for storing property
44. Barracks for storing property
45. Barracks where women's hair was cut
46. Incinerator
47. Former chapel
48. Latrine

Camp III
49. Barracks for Camp III prisoners
50. Barracks for Camp III prisoners' kitchen and "dentist" workshop
51. Gas chambers
52. Engine room for gas chambers
53. Fenced yard
54. Mass graves and outdoor crematoria

Sobibor station and village
55. Railway station
56. Living quarters of Polish railway-workers
57. Houses of local agriculture workers
58. Farms of Polish peasants
59. Living quarter of railway workers

298. Railway station at the Sobibor death camp.

294

299. Ashes and bones at Sobibor after liquidation of the camp.

BELZEC EXTERMINATION CAMP
(Autumn—Winter 1942)

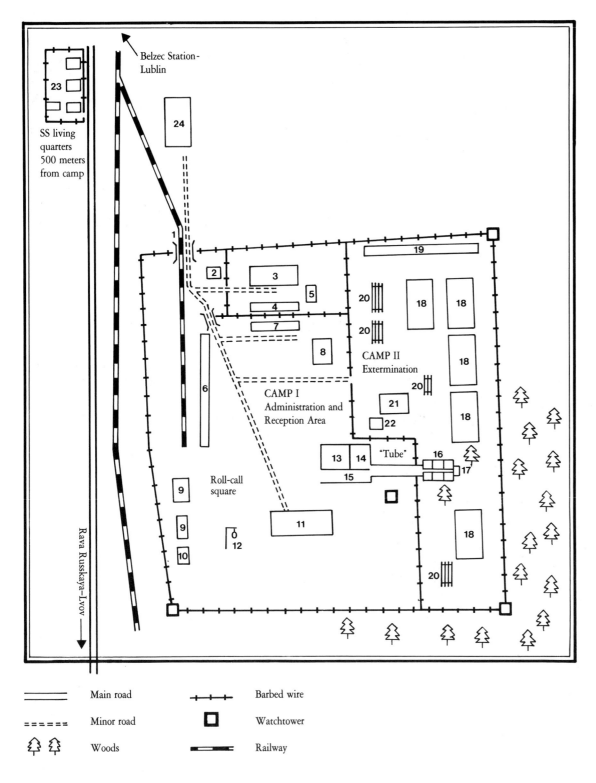

Camp I – Reception and Administration Area

1. Entrance gate
2. Guards' house
3. Ukrainian living quarters
4. Barber, clinic, dentist for the SS and Ukrainian
5. Ukrainian kitchen
6. Railway ramp
7. Garage
8. Tailor's and shoemaker's workshops for the SS and Ukrainians
9. Living quarters for Jewish prisoners
10. Kitchen and laundry for Jewish prisoners
11. Storeroom for belongings taken from victims
12. Gallows
13. Undressing barracks
14. Room in which women's hair was cut
15. A courtyard enclosed by a wooden fence leading to the "tube"

Camp II – Extermination Area

16. Gas chambers
17. Gas engine
18. Burial pits
19. Anti-tank trench used as a burial pit
20. Shelves for cremating the bodies
21. Living quarters for Jewish prisoners
22. Kitchen for Jewish prisoners

Outside the camp

23. The SS living quarters and offices
24. Warehouse for the belongings taken from the victims – former locomotive shed

300

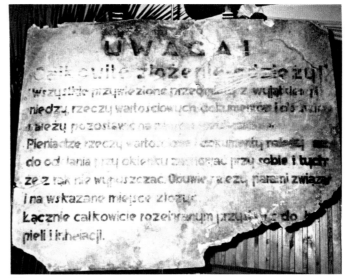

302

JEWISH SONDERKOMMANDO - BEŁZEC DEATH CAMP. 1943

301

300. SS men in the Belzec death camp.

301. Jewish prisoners in the Belzec camp.

302. Sign in the Belzec death camp ordering new arrivals to undress and hand over their money and other valuables before entering the "disinfection and inhalation bath." The Jews were ordered to tie their shoes in pairs and place them in a designated spot. The sign was posted in the arrival yard at the entrance to the camp.

TREBLINKA EXTERMINATION CAMP
Spring 1943

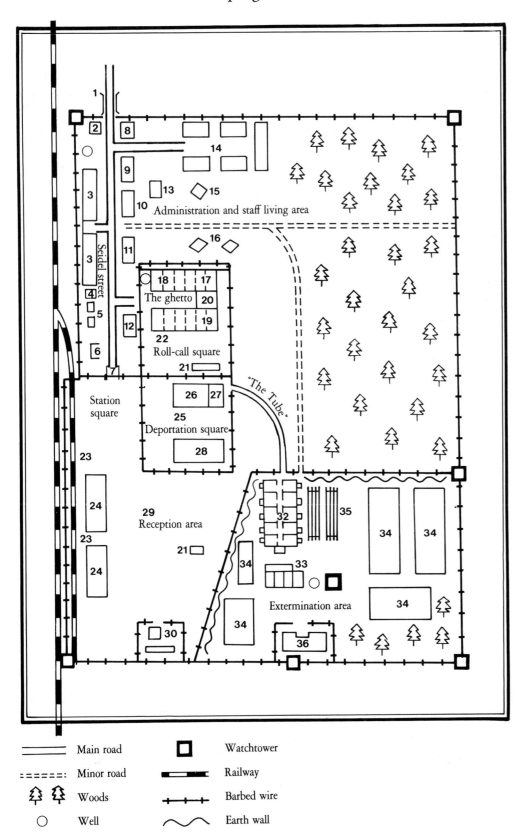

Administration and Staff Living Area

1. Entrance to the camp and Seidel Street
2. Guard's room near the entrance
3. SS living quarters
4. Arms storeroom
5. Gasoline pump and storerooms
6. Garage
7. Entrance gate to Station square
8. Camp Command and Stangl's living quarters
9. Services for SS — barber, sick bay, dentist
10. Living quarters of domestic staff (Polish and Ukrainian girls)
11. Bakery
12. Foodstore and supply storeroom
13. The barrack in which "gold Jews" worked
14. Ukrainian living quarters — "Max Bialas barracks"
15. Zoo
16. Stables, chicken coop, pig pen
17. Living quarters for capos, women, tailor shop, shoe-repairs, carpentry shop and sickroom
18. Prisoners' kitchen
19. Living quarters for men prisoners, prisoners' laundry and tool room
20. Locksmithy and smithy
21. Latrine
22. Roll-call square

Reception Area

23. Station platform (ramp) and square
24. Storeroom for belongings taken from victims — disguised as a station
25. Deportation square
26. Barrack in which the women undressed and relinquished their valuables
27. Room in which women's hair was cut
28. Barrack in which men undressed, also used as a storeroom
29. Reception square
30. "Lazarett" — execution site
31. "The Tube" — the approach to the gas chambers

Extermination Area

32. New gas chambers (10 chambers)
33. Old gas chambers (3 chambers)
34. Burial pits
35. "The Roasts" for burning bodies
36. Prisoners' living quarters, kitchen, and latrines

————	Main road	▣ Watchtower
‥‥‥‥	Minor road	▰ Railway
🌲🌲	Woods	┼┼┼ Barbed wire
○	Well	〰〰 Earth wall

303. Mass grave in Treblinka. It was opened and the bodies burned as part of the German effort to obliterate all traces of their crimes prior to their withdrawal (German photograph taken in 1943).

304. Excavator used for digging huge pits in the Treblinka death camp. Bodies of hundreds of thousands of Jews were burned in these pits.

303

304

305. Chelmno: site of mass graves of Jews.

306. Majdanek, Poland: crematorium.

307, 308. Majdanek, Poland: crematorium.

309. Rollers used for road building which were pulled by prisoners.

310. Tins of Cyclon B poison pellets used in the gas chambers.

307

308

310

311. Mauthausen, Austria: stone quarry.

312

312. Mauthausen concentration camp,
Austria: the prisoners' orchestra plays
while an inmate caught trying to escape
is led to execution.

314

313. Dachau, Germany: prisoners at roll-call.

314. Buchenwald, Germany: torture of prisoners.

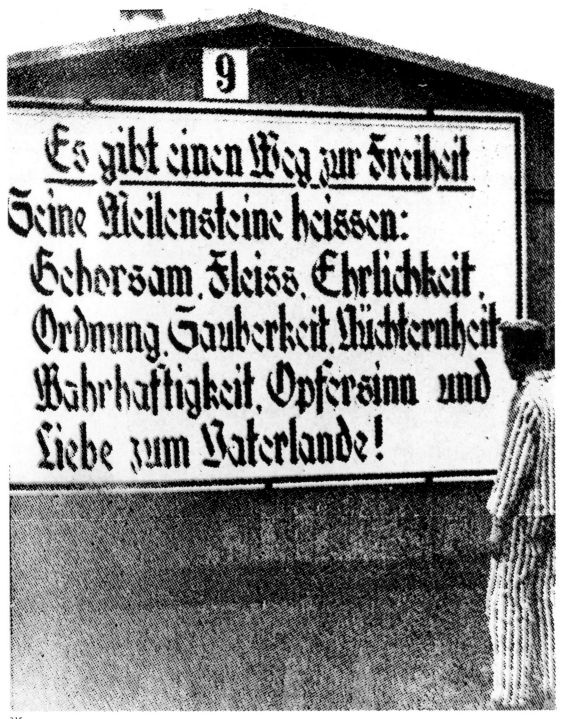

315. Sachsenhausen, Germany: the sign reads: There exists a way to freedom, its milestones are: obedience, diligence, honesty, order, cleanliness, sobriety, truthfulness, self-sacrifice and love for the fatherland.

316. Sachsenhausen, Germany: inmates at forced labor.

317, 318. Jewish inmates at the "appel" (roll call).

317

318

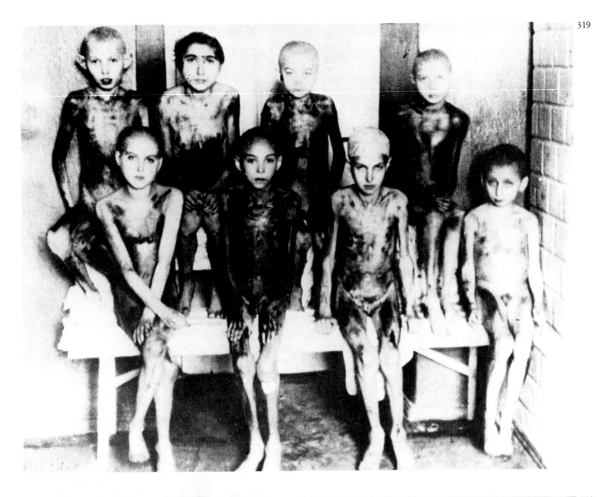

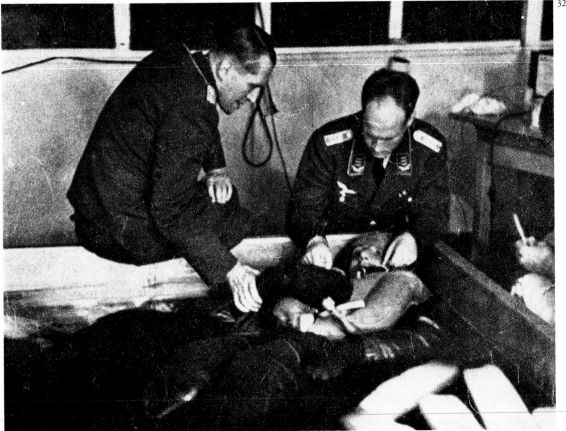

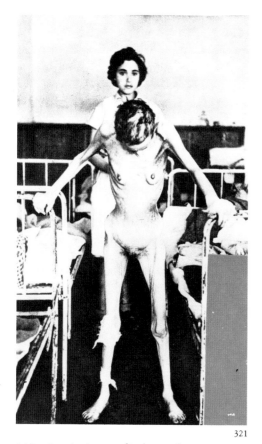

319. Auschwitz: medical experiments on children.

320. Dachau, Germany: medical experiments by Nazi physicians.

321. Female Jewish victims of Nazi medical experiments.

322. Medical experiment on a young boy.

323. Klooga, Estonia, concentration
camp on the eve of the German
withdrawal in September, 1944. Bodies
of Jews were stacked in rows of logs
before being burned as part of the
German effort to erase traces of their
crimes. The Germans did not have time
to burn all the corpses and this photo was
taken immediately after the liberation of
the camp by Soviet troops.

Liquidation of extermination camps

Their task completed, the extermination camps at Belzec, Sobibor and Treblinka, set up for annihilating the Jews in the General Government, were liquidated. Belzec was liquidated first, in the spring of 1943, followed by Treblinka and Sobibor, which was liquidated in mid-October 1943. The camps were dismantled, the area ploughed over, and agricultural farms set up so as to erase completely all traces of the mind-boggling crimes perpetrated on the site. The camp at Chelmno, set up for the purpose of exterminating Jews from the Lodz district, was ultimately liquidated in the early summer of 1944.

In Auschwitz mass extermination continued through the summer of 1944, when transports with Hungarian Jews started arriving. With the entry of the Soviet army into Poland, the Germans had begun preparations in September 1944 for the evacuation of the camp. They included the murder of part of the remaining prisoners, the evacuation of others, and liquidation of the camp to obliterate all traces of what had taken place there. The last transport to be annihilated arrived in Auschwitz on October 28, 1944; it carried 2,000 Jews from Theresienstadt.

The rapid advance of the Red Army forced the Germans to undertake the hasty evacuation of thousands of Auschwitz inmates to Germany. Scores of them died or were shot during the trek in the winter cold. These processions were nicknamed "death marches." The gas chambers and crematoria were blown up by the Germans on the eve of the liberation of the camp by the Soviet army on January 27, 1945. Scores of thousands of prisoners who had survived the evacuation from Auschwitz and other camps were packed into concentration camps in Germany. Most of them died in the terrible conditions which prevailed there before the liberation in March–April 1945.

Reactions in the free world to the murder of Jews

For over six years, from Hitler's assumption of power in 1933 until the outbreak of World War II, the persecution of the Jews in Germany was carried out openly; the whole world stood and watched. The mass media in Germany and abroad reported on the events. The question arises, what was the reaction of the Western powers and other democracies in the world to these events?

In fact, governments of various countries viewed the persecution of Jews in the years 1933–1939 as an internal German affair which did not justify external interference. This attitude was a natural outcome of the policy of appeasement embarked upon by the Western powers toward Germany. They found only one issue difficult to ignore, since it affected their own countries: the question of immigration. Some approach had to be adopted concerning the entry of Jewish refugees from Germany and, after the annexation, from Austria and Czechoslovakia into their countries. Basically their attitude toward immigration was negative. The Western democracies expressed sympathy with the plight of the Jews, but refused to open their gates to large numbers of refugees. Great Britain, which held a Mandate over Palestine and which had pledged to establish a Jewish national home there, went as far as to impose severe restrictions on immigration, even though many Jews sought to enter Palestine.

Public pressure in the western countries led the United States to convene a conference under the auspices of the League of Nations in the French city of Evian. Held in July 1938 and attended by delegates from 32 countries, the Evian Conference was supposed to deliberate the problems of finding sanctuaries for refugees from Germany and from Austria, which three months previously had been annexed to the Third Reich. Great Britain attended on condition that the subject of the immigration of German and Austrian Jews to Palestine would not be included in the agenda. The Conference revealed that no participating government was willing to accept Jewish refugees. It adjourned without any practical resolutions except a proposal to establish an International Refugee Board headquartered in London. However its narrowly-defined jurisdiction and insufficient financing prevented it from rendering effective assistance in solving the refugee problem. Thus the Evian Conference ended in complete failure. The fate of the Jews still remaining in the Third Reich was now completely in the hands of the Nazis who exploited the Conference's failure to the full for their propaganda purposes. They came to the conclusion that the Western powers and other democratic countries did not concern themselves with the fate of German Jewry. German anti-Jewish policies underwent further radicalization and within a few months after the Evian Conference the Nazis unleashed *Kristallnacht*.

After the invasion of Poland, the news of the terror inflicted upon the Jews there and their incarceration in ghettos spread around the world simultaneously with the events or soon thereafter. Information about massacres perpetrated by the Einsatz-gruppen in the occupied areas of the Soviet Union in the second half of 1941, reached the Kremlin and the Polish Underground. The Poles relayed this information to London and Washington. However, it failed to prod the Allies to take any action, or change their policies toward rescuing Jews. The tragic story of the ship "Struma" exemplifies the inflexible attitude and callousness toward Jewish refugees. On December 12, 1941 the "Struma" sailed from the Romanian port of Constantsa under a Panamanian flag, carrying 769 Jews and headed for Palestine. In Constantinople, the Turkish authorities barred its passengers from disembarking, pending British communication allowing their entry into Palestine. The British Mandate authorities in Palestine and in London refused them entry into the Land of Israel. Requests by the Jewish Agency in Jerusalem were turned down and the British refused to allow even the children on the ship to immigrate. On February 23, 1942, the "Struma" was ordered to leave Turkish waters. It sailed back to the Black Sea where it was intercepted and sunk by a Soviet submarine which identified it as an "enemy target."

In the spring and summer of 1942, information reached London and Washington that mass murder of Jews was taking place in extermination camps that had been set up in occupied Poland. Similar information reached the West via the Polish underground and was corroborated by other sources. Swiss representatives of the World

Jewish Congress and the Jewish Agency passed on to London and Washington the information they had received from the German industrialist Eduard Schulte. Thanks to his good relations with key Nazi leaders, Schulte was apprised of the "overall plan to exterminate European Jews" which had been agreed upon by Nazi leaders in Berlin. He passed on this information to Jewish representatives in Switzerland in the summer of 1942. By the late summer and fall of 1942, the Allied powers fighting Nazi Germany had a clear picture of the plan for the total extermination of the Jews in Nazi-occupied Europe and its actual implementation. Henry Morgenthau, the U.S. Secretary of Treasury, wrote in his memoirs: "From August 1942, we in Washington were aware of the Nazi plan to wipe out all European Jews. This notwithstanding, for eighteen months since we had received reports of this monstrous Nazi plan, the State Department did nothing in this matter. . ."

At the end of 1942, London and Washington issued declarations condemning the mass murder of Jews in occupied Europe. At the same time, however, the British ignored demands by Jewish representatives that the British government change or at least mitigate its policy of barring Jews fleeing from occupied countries, particularly from the Balkans, from immigrating to Palestine. The British argued that the question of Jewish refugees must be dealt with in the wider context of all refugees from occupied Europe, despite the fact that Jews lived under a death sentence. In February 1943, the Romanian government proposed to Allied governments to transfer the 70,000 Jews still remaining in Transnistria via the Black Sea to Palestine. Neither Britain nor the United States so much as responded to this proposal.

The pressure of public opinion and of Jewish organizations in the free world to force Germany to halt its murder of Jews and permit their emigration from Europe led to the convening of the Bermuda Conference. From April 19 to 30, 1943, British and U.S. representatives discussed the question of refugees of Nazi-occupied countries. The Conference opened on the day of the beginning of the final liquidation of the Warsaw ghetto. Those present determined that the question of Jewish refugees could not be considered separately from the general refugee problem, and that in view of the military situation no possibility existed of taking active steps to rescue refugees from occupied countries. It was recommended to revive the Refugee Board set up in London after the Evian Conference in 1938. The participants also decided to transfer 20,000 refugees, including 5,000 Jews, from Spain to North Africa.

Shmuel Zygelboym, a major figure in Polish Jewry who had arrived in London from Warsaw as a refugee and acted ceaselessly on behalf of the Jews, took his life two weeks after the Bermuda Conference in protest against inaction in rescuing Jews. In his farewell letter he wrote, *inter alia*: "By my death I wish to make my final protest against the passivity with which the world is looking on and permitting the extermination of the Jewish people."

When transports with hundreds of thousands of Hungarian Jews started rolling toward Auschwitz in 1944, requests were made that the U.S. Air Force bomb the camp installations so as to save at least some of the deportees. Arguing that the Air Force was engaged in bombing raids against military targets, which Auschwitz was not, the Americans turned down these requests.

Not only Britain and the United States refrained from taking direct action to rescue European Jews from extermination. For its part, the Soviet Union took the view that rescue would be best effected by the defeat of Nazi Germany. In fact, throughout the war the Allies took no direct action on behalf of the threatened Jews. Their principal strategic objective, namely the surrender of Germany, accorded with the interests of the Jewish people. But millions of Jews in occupied Europe could not afford to wait for the end of the war as the Nazis were carrying out their extermination plans relentlessly without regard for military developments. The Jewish people paid with the lives of millions of its sons and daughters.

Christian churches

The stance and actions of Christian churches during the Holocaust, particularly the conduct of Pope Pius XII, raises numerous questions: Did they speak out against genocide, against the urder of human beings created in God's image? Did they exert their influence to prevent the murder? Did they call upon their faithful to come to the aid of the persecuted Jew?

By late 1941, the Vatican had already learned through Church channels of the mass executions carried out by the *Einsatzgruppen* in the occupied Soviet Union. When deportations of Slovak Jews to Auschwitz commenced in March 1942, Jewish organizations in Switzerland asked the Pope to intervene in order to halt the deportations. However, the Pope, who carried a great deal of influence with the Slovak government headed by a Catholic priest, Jozef Tiso, refrained from taking action. As early as the summer and fall of 1942, the Vatican also received information from reliable sources about the death camps, mass murder in occupied Poland, and plans to deport hundreds of thousands of European Jews there. However, apart from general pronouncements about "war atrocities," the Pope kept silent. He did not raise his voice to exhort the faithful to observe the commandment "Thou shall not murder." The assistance rendered by the Vatican to the Jews of Rome during their deportation in October 1943, was an exception rather than the rule.

In contrast to the Pope's silence, it should be noted that in several places in Europe, such as France and the Netherlands, Catholic and Protestant clergy did speak out and take action on behalf of the Jews. Priests of the Greek Orthodox Church in Bulgaria and Greece did likewise. The limited scope of these efforts only throws into relief what could have been done. It is noteworthy that among the "Righteous among the Nations" honored by Yad Vashem in Jerusalem, there are many priests who, acting on their own and answering the call of the moral imperative, came to the aid of the Jews at a time of unprecedented ordeal. The historical account and moral reckoning of the behavior of Christian churches during the Holocaust has yet to be made.

JEWISH ARMED RESISTANCE
IN OCCUPIED EUROPE

324. Warsaw ghetto going up in flames.

JEWISH ARMED RESISTANCE IN OCCUPIED EUROPE

Jewish armed resistance in occupied Europe

Armed resistance by Jews in occupied Europe was a widespread phenomenon, encompassing a broad range of action. Although it occurred wherever there were Jews under the rule of the Nazis or their satellites, Eastern Europe was the main scene of armed struggle. In many places the Jewish fighting underground constituted a direct extension of the political underground which came into being shortly after the beginning of German occupation. In every country Jewish resistance had to adapt itself to local conditions and realities as it endeavored to cope with the problems that Nazi policies posed for Jews. In many ghettos and death camps of Eastern Europe, Jews began to organize armed resistance against the Germans. Wherever the terrain was suitable for guerilla warfare, Jewish partisans operated. In Western Europe, where conditions were not suitable for armed struggle and, at the same time, some opportunities for rescue existed, the Jewish underground devoted its main efforts to hiding Jews among the local population and smuggling them across the border to Spain and Switzerland.

The beginning of armed resistance coincided with the onset of the physical annihilation of the Jews, shortly after the invasion of the Soviet Union. Although nuclei of resistance sprang up in several places, the first ideologically-inspired organization with plans for armed resistance was set up in the Vilna ghetto. In January 1942, various political groupings active in the ghetto, such as the Zionists, Bundists and Communists, joined together to form the United Partisans Organization (F.P.O.). Underground fighting organizations were also set up in the ghettos of Minsk, Warsaw, Bialystok, Krakow and Kovno, as well as in other larger and smaller ghettos. Under conditions of nearly total isolation and lack of communication between the various ghettos, the organization of resistance was the result of local initiative, usually instigated by members of the Zionist youth movements.

Fighting organizations began to form without any direction or coordination from above. In the Warsaw ghetto in the General Government, the Jewish Combat Organization (*Zydowska Organizacja Bojowa* — Z.O.B.) came into being, it included members of the Zionist *Hehalutz* youth movement, the Bund and the Communists, as well as the Jewish Military Union (Z.Z.W.), consisting mostly of Revisionist Zionists.

Among all sections of the Jewish public, the underground was the first to realize that the purpose of the deportations was not "resettlement of Jews" or "transfer to labor camps," as the Germans alleged, but total extermination. The information it gathered came from Jews who had escaped from the killing sites in the East where the notorious *Einsatzgruppen* operated, and later, from escapees from the death camps of Treblinka, Chelmno and others. This information received independent corroboration from non-Jewish underground organizations with which the Jewish organizations maintained contact, particularly in Warsaw.

The Jewish underground sought to tear down the veil of secrecy with which the Germans had enveloped the mass murder of Jews and to reveal the facts both to the Jewish and non-Jewish world. They hoped that by throwing light on the ongoing genocide, they would enable at least some Jews to evade deportation, and find refuge among the local non-Jewish population. They also hoped that alerting the world to the heinous crimes perpetrated against the Jewish people would bring pressure to bear on the Germans to halt the killings.

Emissaries and couriers dispatched by the Jewish underground, mostly young women who could easily pass as non-Jews, travelled from one ghetto to another, passing on information about the extermination and issuing calls to organize armed resistance. In many ghettos these reports were received sceptically; their residents simply refused to believe that the Nazis were engaged in wiping out a whole people for no specific reason. But even those who believed it were aware of the limited opportunities for rescue due to the unwillingness of the majority of the local inhabitants to imperil themselves by sheltering the persecuted Jews.

The Jewish underground determined that its principal aim would be armed struggle against the Nazis, either by means of an uprising in the ghetto or by partisan combat in the woods. The first prerequisite in such a struggle was the procurement of weapons, but for the Jews it was difficult to acquire them. There were many weapons left behind by the Polish army after its surrender in September 1939, as well as by the Red Army in the course of its retreat eastward in the second half of 1941. These arms were collected and hidden by the local inhabitants. Weapons from this source could be purchased at exorbitant prices, but this meant having to find the sellers and obtain the funds. Contacting unknown persons for the purpose of purchasing weapons entailed great risks. The would-be seller was liable to inform the Germans, or take the money without delivering the goods while threatening denunciation. Since conditions ruled out the testing of weapons to be purchased, the underground often bought weapons which turned out to be unusable. In the various ghettos, clandestine workshops were set up to

325. Mordecai Anielewicz, commander of the Warsaw ghetto uprising.

326. Yitzhak Zuckerman, "Antek," deputy commander of the Warsaw ghetto uprising.

325

326

repair old and broken-down weapons purchased outside. These workshops also manufactured side-arms, primitive grenades, and incendiary bombs (Molotov cocktails).

The Jewish underground also attempted to obtain weapons from non-Jewish resistance organizations which commanded large stockpiles, mainly in occupied Poland. However, with few exceptions, the requests for arms were turned down. It is noteworthy that in addition to the existing stockpiles, the non-Jewish underground also received weapons through parachute drops from Britain, where many governments-in-exile functioned, or from the Soviet Union. The Jewish underground was the only resistance organization in occupied Europe to receive no arms whatsoever from these sources.

Purchasing weapons and stockpiling them in the ghetto presented the Jewish underground with an acute moral dilemma. For although the ghettos were doomed under the sentence of the "final solution" regardless of the actions of their residents, amassing weapons imperiled the ghetto in the short term. Upon learning of the existence of armed resistance organizations engaged in planning an uprising or joining the partisans, the Germans were liable to advance the date of liquidation. Furthermore, the Germans applied the principle of collective responsibility, according to which all ghetto residents were held accountable for the actions of individuals. Consequently, members of underground resistance organizations were obliged to take all necessary precautions in purchasing weapons, smuggling them in, and stockpiling them in the ghetto.

Despite all the difficulties and risks, Jewish resistance organizations managed to procure arms, although the quantities were far from adequate. In fact, the shortage of weapons was one of the principal factors which limited the scope of Jewish armed resistance in Nazi-occupied Europe.

Uprisings in the ghettos were not aimed at defeating the Germans, as this was well beyond the means and strength of the Jewish resisters. Nor could the rescue of thousands of ghetto residents be contemplated. The uprisings broke out when underground leaders saw the liquidation coming, at which point the Jews had nothing to lose. Uprisings amounted to a last stand, a fight for Jewish honor, not letting the Germans carry out their plans of extermintion without any resistance. Or, as one of the fighters put it, "to merit three lines in the history books." A secondary objective was to exploit the disorder and commotion created by the fighting so as to break through the encirclement, reach the woods, and join partisan units operating there, but very few among the fighters could hope to embark on such a plan under the prevailing conditions.

The largest uprising broke out in the Warsaw ghetto on April 19, 1943, following the German decision to undertake the final liquidation of the ghetto. In fact, the Warsaw ghetto uprising was the first mass revolt against the Nazis in the whole of occupied Europe. The uprising was led by the Jewish Combat Organization (Z.O.B.), under the command of Mordecai Anielewicz, and the Jewish Military Union

(Z.Z.W.). Groups of ghetto residents unaffiliated with these two organizations also took part in the fighting. The initial German attempts to break into the ghetto were beaten off, with the attackers leaving behind dead and wounded. The Germans responded by changing their tactics. They employed heavy cannons to shell the ghetto and began to systematically burn and blow up the ghetto buildings with their residents inside. After several weeks of unequal battle which pitted Jewish fighters armed with Molotov cocktails and revolvers against cannons, heavy machine guns and tanks, the ghetto was defeated. A majority of the fighters died in battle. On May 8, the Germans blew up the bunker housing the headquarters of the Jewish Combat Organization. About one hundred fighters, including Mordehai Anielewicz, were killed. Scores of Warsaw ghetto residents died under the rubble or burned to death in the raging inferno. The survivors were deported to the camps of Trawniki, Poniatowa and Majdanek.

Uprisings broke out in other ghettos too. In the Bialystok ghetto an uprising began on August 16, 1943, and after hours of fighting it was finally overwhelmed on August 18. Most of the fighters died in combat. The surviving remnants managed to break through and reach the woods where they joined the partisans. In the Vilna ghetto the Germans clashed with the underground Jewish resisters on September 1, 1943. After the battle a few hundred underground fighters left the ghetto for the woods of Narocz and Rudniki, where they proceeded to organize a Jewish partisan movement. Uprisings and armed resistance against the Germans also took place in Czestochowa, Bedzin, Brody, Krakow, Tuczyn, Nieswiez and in other ghettos and concentration camps.

Jews also rose up against the Germans in the death camps. Thus on October 22 1942 a group of Jewish prisoners in the Sachsenhausen camp revolted when it became known to them that they were going to be sent to Auschwitz. The SS guards succeeded in quelling the uprising and all the prisoners who took part in the rebellion were executed. On August 2, 1943, Jewish prisoners revolted in the extermination camp at Treblinka, and on October 14 an uprising broke out in Sobibor. Underground organizations in these camps had been preparing resistance for many months. On the day of the uprising in Treblinka, the resisters attacked the SS men, wounding a number of them. In Sobibor most of the SS men were killed during the revolt. The fighters seized their weapons and hundreds of prisoners fled by breaking through the fence. Most of the prisoners died in fighting or during the escape, but several dozen in each of the two camps succeeded in reaching the woods and joining partisans there. On October 7, 1944, members of the *Sonderkommando* who serviced the gas chambers in Auschwitz, revolted. They blew up some of the gas chambers and killed several SS men. Nearly all of them died in the uprising; a handful succeeded in escaping.

Understandably, partisan movements came into being mainly in those Nazi-occupied countries with suitable topography: vast stretches of forests, barely accessible mountainous areas, etc. Thus, broadly-based partisan movements evolved in the course

327

328

327. Arye Rodal, commander of the underground Jewish Military Union in the Warsaw ghetto.

328. "There is no more a Jewish residential quarter in Warsaw". Report of the commander of the German forces attacking the Warsaw ghetto.

329. Mordecai Tennenbaum, commander of the underground uprising in the Bialystok ghetto.

329

of 1942 and early 1943 in the occupied areas of the Soviet Union with their huge expanses of forests, in the mountains of Yugoslavia, and in later stages and on a smaller scale, in eastern Poland, certain regions of Slovakia, France and Greece. Due to the fact that the mass killing of Jews occurred in these areas prior to the development of any significant partisan warfare, only those Jews who had survived the waves of extermination became partisans. Furthermore, in Eastern Europe both the latent and manifest anti-Semitism prevalent among broad sections of the local populations made it very difficult for these surviving Jews to set up their own partisan units. Consequently, Jews could live in the woods and operate as partisans only in areas where non-Jewish partisan movements operated and where these partisans agreed to accept Jews in their ranks. At any rate, Jews were received only on the condition that they would bring their own arms. In exceptional cases they were able to form and deploy their own partisan units operating in tandem with non-Jewish units.

Another problem facing Jewish partisans were a variety of bands and partisan formations affiliated with anti-Semitic movements. These were especially active in the forests of Eastern Europe. They did not shrink from massacring Jewish partisans or Jewish families seeking refuge in the woods.

In the years 1942–43, a growing number of Jews from the ghettos began joining Soviet partisans operating in the forests of Western Byelorussia, northern parts of the Western Ukraine, and Eastern Lithuania. Scattered throughout the forests of this region were also camps with Jewish families, some of them under the auspices of the Soviet partisan movement. Various estimates put the number of Jews in Soviet partisan formations at 25,000 to 30,000, i.e., roughly 10% of the total partisan strength in this region. In the forests of Eastern Poland, the partisan formations of the *Armia Krajowa* (the Home Army — the largest political and military underground organization in Poland) in general, and right-wing Polish groupings in particular, tended to display hostility to Jewish partisans. Only the numerically small formations of the left-wing *Armia Ludowa* (People's Army) accepted Jews into their ranks. Altogether, several thousand Jewish partisans were active in the Polish forests. Frequently they had to conceal their identities and assume non-Jewish-sounding *noms de guerre*.

Like their non-Jewish comrades, Jewish partisans launched assaults on German garrisons, laid ambushes, mined railways and roads, and took revenge on German soldiers and collaborators.

Hundreds of thousands of Jewish soldiers fought in the ranks of Allied armies on all war fronts. They fought on land, in the air, and at sea, on war fronts in Eastern and Western Europe, in North Africa, and in the Near and Far East. The Jewish community in the Land of Israel, which at that time numbered half a million people, sent 28,000 volunteers to serve in the British army. Thus the Jewish people had a part in the victory over Nazi Germany.

330

330. German heavy machineguns firing into the Warsaw ghetto.

331. Emmanuel Ringelblum, historian, organizer of the Warsaw ghetto's underground archives.

332. Warsaw ghetto: man jumping from the window of a burning house.

333. Warsaw ghetto: Germans setting fire to houses.

331

332

333

335

334. Warsaw ghetto: a group of Jews captured in the ghetto during the uprising.

335. Warsaw ghetto: A group of Jews captured in the ghetto during the uprising. The white tags on their clothes mark them as employees of a German industrial enterprise.

336. Warsaw ghetto: a group of Jews captured in the ghetto during the uprising.

337. Warsaw ghetto: Members of the Jewish Combat Organization after their capture.

336

338. Warsaw ghetto: inhabitants captured during the uprising.

339

340

341

339, 340. Warsaw ghetto: inhabitants captured during the uprising.

341. Warsaw ghetto: a group of Jewish fighters before their execution. They had been flushed out of their bunker hideouts by the Germans.

342. Warsaw ghetto: a group of Jewish
fighters before their execution.

PARTISANS

343

344

343. Jewish partisans from the Kovno ghetto photographed in the Rudniki forest, where they operated.

344. Mines planted by Jewish partisans derailed dozens of German trains like this one, which transported soldiers and equipment to the front.

345. Haim Yellin, commander of the Jewish underground in the Kovno ghetto.

346. Jewish partisans from the Kovno ghetto photographed in the Rudniki forest, where they operated.

345

347. A group of Jewish partisans from Vilna after the liberation of the city, July, 1944. Among others in the photograph: Abba Kovner, commander of the Jewish underground in the Vilna ghetto (fourth from right); Vitka Kempner (first from right); Reizl (Ruszka) Korczak (third from right); Elhanan Maggid (first from left).

348. A group of Jewish partisans from the Vilna ghetto who took part in the battles for the liberation of the Vilna district.

347

348

349

350

351

352

353

349. Abba Kovner, leader of the Vilna ghetto underground after Wittenberg's death.

350. Ilya Ehrenburg with Vilna ghetto underground fighters after the liberation of Vilna.

351. Yitzhak Wittenberg, commander of the Vilna ghetto underground.

352. Josef Glazman, one of the leaders of the Vilna ghetto underground.

353. Yehiel Scheinbaum, leader of an underground group in the Vilna ghetto.

354. Jewish partisans Yitzhak Rudnicki (Arad) and Motke Bushkanietz in the Kozyany woods.

355. A group of Jewish partisans from Swieciany, eastern Lithuania; members of the "Vilnus" partisan unit. First from right, Feibl Hayat; second from right, Jozef Flexer; sixth from right, Shimon Iskin.

356, 357. Decoration (class one) and certificate awarded to "Partisan of the Great Patriotic War" Yitzhak Rudnicki (Arad) by the president of the Supreme Soviet of the Lithuanian Soviet Republic for his activities against the Germans.

358. Rachel Rudnicki, a Jewish woman partisan in the Rudniki forest south of Vilna. This photo was published in a Soviet newspaper immediately after the liberation. The title reads: partisan from Lithuania.

359. Berl-Boris Yohai, a Jewish partisan, planting mines under railway tracks (Swieciany, Eastern Lithuania).

354

355

356

ВРЕМЕННОЕ УДОСТОВЕРЕНИЕ № 46718

Предъявитель сего *Рудницкий*
(фамилия)

Исаак Моисеевич
(имя и отчество) *Президиума Верховного*

Награжден приказом начальника _____ штаба

Совета СССР

партизанского движения № _____ от „ *14* " *сентября* 1944 г

за доблесть и мужество, проявленные в партизанской

борьбе против немецко-фашистских захватчиков

медалью „Партизану отечественной войны"

X степени медаль № _____

Начальник _____ штаба
партизанского движения

Председатель Президиума Верховного Совета Литовской ССР
Подпись вручающего
(должность и фамилия)
м. п.

24 ___ *февраля* ___ 1945 г (*Ю. Палецкис*)

ПАРТИЗАНЫ ЛИТВЫ

360. Jewish partisans in Western Byelorussia, July, 1941. From left to right: Sevek (Severin) Rosen, Shalom Holavski, Kantorowicz.

361. Shalom Zorin, commander of a Jewish partisan unit and the family camp from the Minsk ghetto.

363

364

362. Tuvia Bielski, commander of a
Jewish partisan unit and the family camp
in the Nalibok forest (Byelorussia).

363, 364. Father and son, David and
Shmuel Bobrow, Jewish partisans in the
Nalibok forest (Byelorussia).

365. A group of Jewish partisans in a
family camp.

365

366

366. A partisan ambush.

367. He, too, fought in the woods.

368. Jewish partisans in battle.

369. Jewish partisans in the woods of Polesia with families.

368

367

369

370. Jewish partisans in the woods of the Lublin district, Poland.

371. A partisan unit under the command of Yehiel Grynszpan was incorporated in the Polish "Armiya Ludowa."

372. Djadja ("uncle") Misha, Moshe Gilderman, commander of a Jewish partisan unit in the Ukraine.

373. Major Alexander Skotnicki, commander of a Jewish partisan unit incorporated in the Polish "Armiya Lodowa" who fell in battle, May, 1944.

376

374. Jewish woman, belonging to the French resistance, being tried by the Vichy authorities in 1942, following the discovery of a Jewish resistance group after explosives they were preparing blew up in their hideout.

375. A group of Jewish partisans in France. From left to right: Jean-Jaques Freyman, Jacques Lazarus, Patricia Gras (crouching), Henri Broder, Pierre Loele, Albert Cohen.

376. A German military vehicle ambushed by partisans.

377

377. A Jewish partisan unit on the island of Rab (Yugoslavia) after the liberation of the island by Yugoslav partisans, 1943.

378. Marshal Yosip Broz Tito, commander of the Yugoslav partisans and Mosha Pijade, a Jew, subsequently became Vice President of Yugoslavia.

379. Jewish partisans in Macedonia, Yugoslavia.

380

380, 381. A group of Jewish and non-Jewish partisans in Macedonia, Yugoslavia.

382. Jews among Greek partisans, Thebes, July 1944. On the left Louis Cohen; on the right David Broido.

381

383. Parachutists from Eretz Israel behind German lines in Yugoslavia with a unit of Yugoslav partisans. Third from left: Reuven Dafni; seventh from left: Hannah Szenes; next to her crouching, Abba Berdichev; on the extreme right: Jonah Rosen.

384–390. Parachutists from Eretz Israel dropped behind German lines in Europe. In March/April, 1944, 32 parachutists were dropped over Italy and the Balkans. Their chief mission was to rescue Jews. Some were captured and executed, others fell in combat during the suppression of the Slovakian uprising. Hannah Szenes landed in Yugoslavia, crossed the Hungarian border and was captured and subsequently executed. Haviva Reik, Zvi Ben-Yaakov, Raphael Reiss and Abba Berdichev died in combat in Slovakia. Enzo Sereni was captured in Italy and executed in Dachau. Peretz Goldstein was captured in Hungary and killed in Mauthausen.

384. Hannah Szenes
385. Zvi Ben-Yaakov
386. Raphael Reis
387. Havivah Reik
388. Enzo Sereni
389. Peretz Goldstein
390. Abba Berdichev

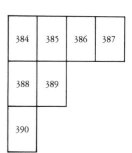

384	385	386	387
388	389		
390			

391. Hanging of two partisans in Minsk,
October 1941. On the left: 17-year-old
Jewess Masha Bruskina.

END OF THE WAR

392. Child survivors of Auschwitz on the
day of liberation in January 1945,
photographed by Soviet soldiers who
liberated the camp.

END OF THE WAR

With the entry of the United States into the war, the battle of Stalingrad, and the invasion of Italy, the tide of war turned in favor of the Allies. On June 6, 1944, the armies of the Western Allies landed large forces in Normandy on the coast of France. Within the next few months they liberated France and reached the German border. Following a number of mass offensives on the Eastern front, Soviet armies approached German soil. Nazi Germany faced total defeat. A huge offensive launched in the first months of 1945 both in the East and West ended with the conquest of Berlin on May 1, 1945. Germany capitulated and on May 8 it surrendered unconditionally. World War II and the bloody rule of the Nazis ended.

During the liberation of concentration and extermination camps, soldiers of the Allied armies stood aghast at the horror. They came across huge piles of corpses at the camps, mass graves, warehouses brimming over with clothing, personal belongings and human hair. The emaciated and starved camp inmates appeared as walking skeletons. Many of them were dying and scores died after the liberation despite the efforts to save them.

Most Jews who survived the Holocaust, including those who had hidden with the help of righteous Gentiles, partisans, and camp survivors, as well as refugees who returned from the Soviet Union, refused to return to their destroyed homes and to renew their lives in exile on soil drenched with Jewish blood. Those who did return often encountered anger and open hostility on the part of the local inhabitants. In the first months after the liberation, a number of survivors in Eastern European countries were murdered by anti-Semitic bands and all kinds of "inheritors" of Jewish property. On July 4, 1946, in the city of Kielce in Poland, a mob staged a pogrom against the Jews, murdering 47 Jews and wounding over 50 out of a total of some 200 survivors who had come back to the city. Murders of Jews, although on a smaller scale, also took place in other localities in Poland, Lithuania, the Ukraine and other places.

Many survivors made their way to Western and Southern Europe, hoping to reach Eretz Israel. In the years 1944–48, Jewish organizations from Palestine organized a vast venture known as *Berikha* and *Haapalah* (escape and "illegal" immigration). Holocaust survivors played a major role in this operation. The British authorities continued their policy of preventing Jews from immigrating to Eretz Israel. Small and ramshackle boats filled with Holocaust survivors repeatedly broke through the British blockade and reached the shores of Israel. However, many of them were caught and interned in camps in Cyprus where the British kept them until May 15, 1948, the day of the establishment of the State of Israel. Some survivors lost their lives in trying to reach Eretz Israel. Holocaust survivors played an important role in the struggle for the establishment of an independent Jewish state, which became the home for many of them. There they successfully rebuilt their homes and families. There they reconfirmed the ancient adage: "Am Yisrael Hay" (The People of Israel Live).

393

394

393. Soviet physician examining an
Auschwitz inmate after the liberation.

394. Liberated prisoners.

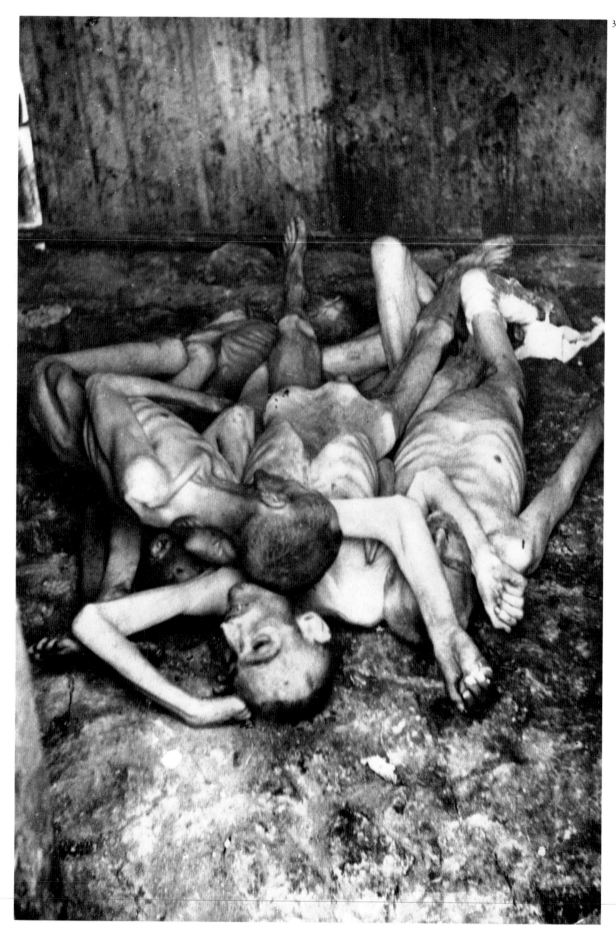

396

395. Bodies of murdered Jews in
Dachau.

396. Bodies of prisoners in the Dachau
concentration camp.

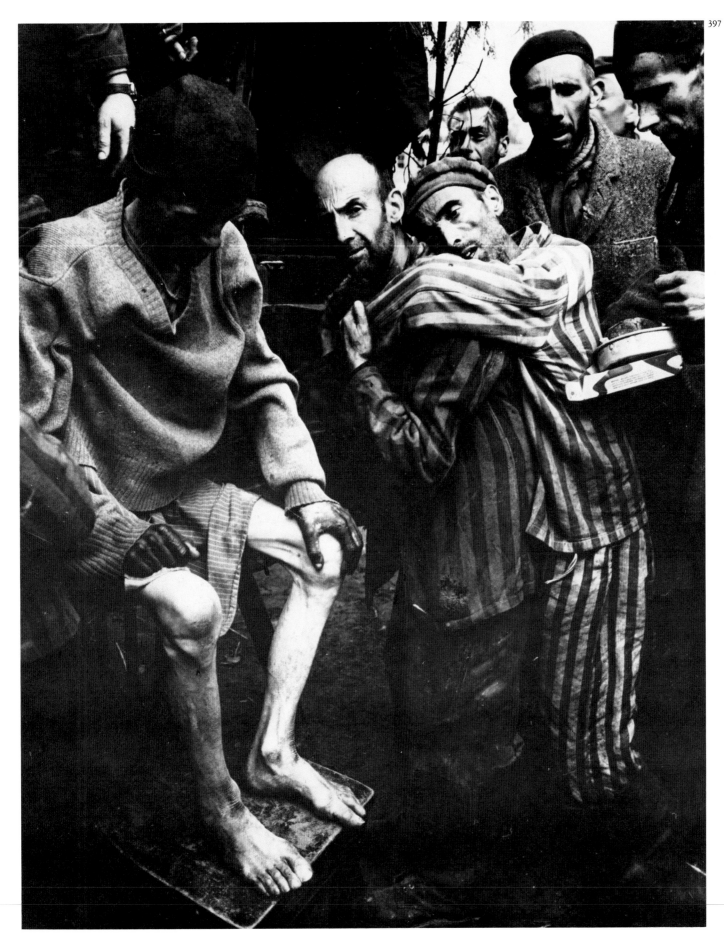

398

397, 398. Wöbbelin concentration camp,
Germany, after liberation by American
troops.

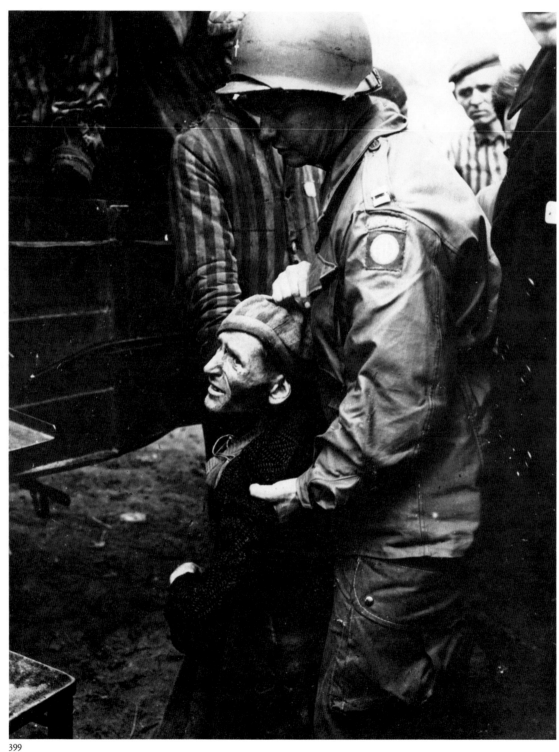

399

400

399, 400. Wöbbelin: liberated prisoners
being taken to hospital.

401

401. Wöbbelin: an American soldier
checking a prisoner who had died on the
road after liberation.

402. Survivors of Flossenberg
concentration camp after their liberation.

403. Buchenwald, after the Liberation: survivors in their barracks. Elie Wiesel, Nobel Peace Prize winner, 1986, is the farthest right on the second tier from below.

404. Buchenwald after liberation.

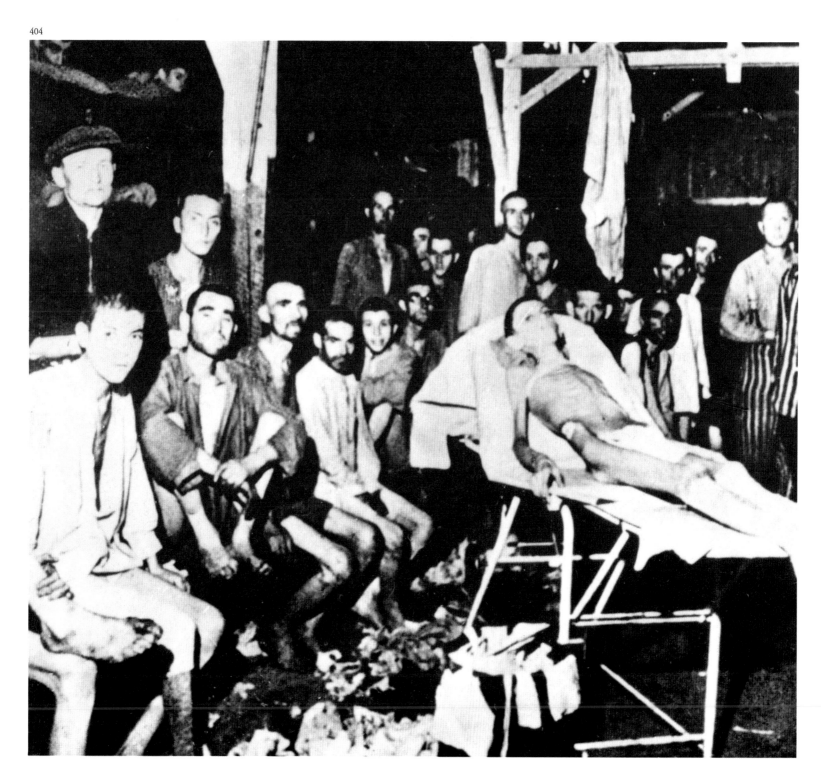

405

405. Bergen-Belsen concentration camp:
a survivor.

406. Bergen Belsen: women survivors
after the liberation.

406

THIS IS THE SITE OF
THE INFAMOUS BELSEN CONCENTRATION CAMP
Liberated by the British on 15 april 1945.

10,000 UNBURIED DEAD WERE FOUND HERE,
ANOTHER 13,000 HAVE SINCE DIED,
ALL OF THEM VICTIMS OF THE
GERMAN NEW ORDER IN EUROPE,
AND AN EXAMPLE OF NAZI KULTUR.

408

407. Bergen Belsen: a mass grave.

408. Bergen Belsen: sign posted by British soldiers.

409. Bergen Belsen: survivors after the liberation (overleaf).

407

410. Bergen Belsen: female SS guards forced to bury the bodies of prisoners after liberation of the camp by the British.

411. A liberated prisoner points an accusing finger toward a Nazi guard.

412. Bergen Belsen: liberated Jewish women survivors dragging corpses of murdered victims to a mass grave (overleaf).

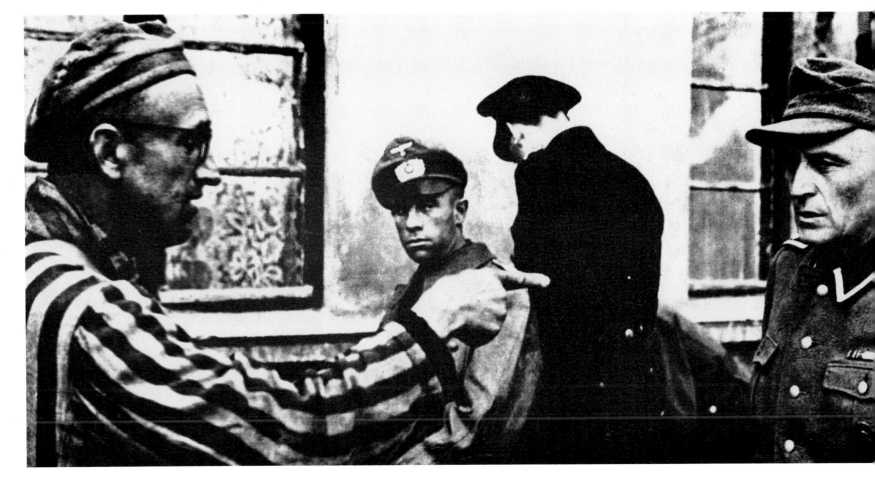

413. Wöbbelin: German civilians forced to carry murdered inmates of the Neuenburg concentration camp for burial, by order of the American army.

EN ROUTE TO ISRAEL

414. Liberated children still kept behind barbed wire.

415. The joy of liberation.

416, 417. Liberated Jewish orphans
being assembled for emigration to
Palestine (Eretz Israel).

418. Jewish survivors attempting to cross
European borders (illegally) in a bid to
reach Palestine (Eretz Israel).

416

417

418

419

420

419. Jewish survivors attempting to cross European borders (illegally) en route for Palestine (Eretz Israel).

420. "The Jewish State," a ship bringing Jewish survivors to Palestine (Eretz Israel) after capture by the British navy, October, 1946.

421. The former Canadian corvette "Joshua Wedgewood" with 1,300 European Jewish refugees aboard, captured by British warships near the shores of Palestine, 27 July, 1946.

422. The sign on the SS Joshua Wedgewood reads: "We survived Hitler. Death is no stranger to us. Nothing can keep us from our Jewish Homeland. Our blood will be on your head if you fire on an unarmed ship."

423. British detention camp in Cyprus, 1947.

424

424. The 'illegal' ship "Theodor Herzl" captured by the British navy on April 14, 1947. The sign reads: "The Germans destroyed our families and homes. Don't you destroy our hope."

425. The 'illegal' ship "Haim Arlosorov with refugees on board beached itself near Haifa. British soldiers are visible in the foreground and British warships in the background. February, 1947 (overleaf).